Famous
Hebrew Christians

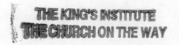

Famous
Hebrew Christians

Jacob Gartenhaus

Baker Book House
Grand Rapids, Michigan

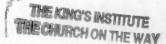

Copyright 1979 by
Baker Book House Company
ISBN: 0-8010-3733-6

Printed in the United States of America
Illustrations by Allen Wallace

TO

all those Jewish believers in the time of Christ and His Apostles, who were the Christian church and were the foundation of the greater church which grew from their witness, and to those Hebrew Christians in every age and in every land who have borne their witness to Christ and have suffered the reproach of Christ at the hands of their fellow Jews—"a multitude which no man can number"—and whose names are written in the Lamb's Book of Life, this volume is gratefully dedicated.

Contents

Foreword

Few people realize the impact that great Hebrew Christians have made upon the religious world. Most of us have read the autobiographies of the noted Gentile pastors and evangelists of past centuries with great interest, but we have failed to recognize that in the last nineteen hundred years Hebrew Christians of great stature have paid an unbelievably high price to make their stand for Jesus Christ. Through their preaching and writing, multitudes have been led to Him.

Dr. Jacob Gartenhaus, one of the most unique men I have ever met, is a Hebrew Christian whose written works are widely acclaimed by many religious leaders of our day. In many respects his new work, *Famous Hebrew Christians,* will be one of the most helpful books he has published. The history of Jewish Christians in modern days has been sorely neglected, and this edition by Dr. Gartenhaus, who has spent his life seeking to reach his Jewish friends for Christ, will fill a great void.

I am sure every serious preacher will want this volume in his library, and will study it with great profit. And, because of the historical value of this volume, it should be in the library of every Bible school, Christian college, and seminary in the

country. The book is a masterpiece, and it is my hope and
prayer that it will receive a wide distribution throughout the
Christian world.

Dr. W. E. Dowell
President, Baptist Bible Fellowship

Foreword

I rejoice that God has spared my friend, Dr. Jacob Gartenhaus, and enabled him to complete this valuable book, which will be a distinctive contribution to Christian biography.

Dr. Gartenhaus is certainly qualified to write this book, for he is one of the world's best-known Hebrew Christians. He has ministered faithfully both to Jews and to Gentiles for over sixty years, and has proved his deep love for Israel and for the church. His ministry has taken him around the world, where he has worked with many different groups of Christians. This is one reason he writes with such breadth of vision, and avoids narrowness and prejudice.

It is vital that all Christians understand the rich heritage the church has in these famous Hebrew Christians. How much we owe to them, and to their descendants today! May the Lord help us all to feel the spiritual debt that we have "both to the Jews and to the Greeks"—and may we begin to pay that debt by sharing the gospel of Jesus Christ with the lost souls who so desperately need it.

Dr. Warren W. Wiersbe
Chicago, Illinois

Acknowledgments

I desire to acknowledge indebtedness for much information concerning the subjects of the following biographical sketches to various standard histories and encyclopedias, and from several magazines and periodicals, particularly the following: The Jewish Encyclopedia; Heinrich Graetz' History of the Jews; Juden Mission, by the Rev. J. F. de le Roi; The Talmud; The Hebrew Christian Witness, by Rev. Dr. Moses Margoliouth; Jewish Witnesses for Christ, by R. A. Bernstein; Sites and Scenes, by Rev. W. T. Gidney; Gethsemane in Our Lives, by B. A. M. Shapiro; Witnesses from Israel (life stories of Jewish converts to Christianity) edited by Rev. Arnold Frank; The History of the London Society for Promoting Christianity Among the Jews, by the Rev. W. T. Gidney; Memories of Gospel Triumphs Among the Jews During the Victorian Era, by Rev. John Dunlop; and The Jewish Herald, a record of the work of the British Society for the Propagation of the Gospel Among the Jews.

—J.G.

Note to Jewish Readers

I want to emphasize to Jews who are biased against the so-called *Meshumadim* (a derogatory term applied to Jews who accept Christ as Messiah and Savior) that, with few exceptions, Jews who acknowledge Jesus Christ as Lord become better Jews. They do not abandon their Jewishness or Judaism; they merely pass from the purely traditional Judaism to the pure and completed Judaism realized in Christ.

Jews who have become Christians have brought honor and credit to the Jewish people, and have dispelled much of the prejudice and hatred directed against the Jews.[1] The names of

---

1. In the Middle Ages, some so-called converts from among the Jews did cause their fellow Jews much suffering. But their attitudes and behavior might well have been a reaction to the bigotry and animosity directed against them by their fellow Jews, who generally oppressed and ill-used those of their people whom they judged to be *Meshumadim*. Also, many leaders and spokesmen of the Church, who should have been examples of Christian charity and enlightenment, were in fact corrupt and evil. The few Jewish converts who did cause fellow Jews to suffer were not good Jews, and they were worse Christians. They were not *Meshumadim* ("renegade" Jews), they were renegade Christians. The gospel of Christ should have inspired them to love every man, particularly their fellow Jews.

such Hebrew Christians form a glorious roll of honor of which the Jewish people might justifiably be proud. Among them are such men as Benjamin Disraeli; Felix Mendelssohn; Alfred Edersheim; Augustus Neander; Isaac da Costa; Joseph Schereschewsky; Isaac Salkinson; David Ginsburg; and many others. These all, and a great host of Jewish believers, have borne a praiseworthy testimony by their lives and work to the great genius of the Jewish people. And this would have been impossible if they had remained within the spiritual ghetto of their Jewish contemporaries.

It is unfortunate that there are Jewish leaders who exert much effort, and spend much money, in the perpetuation of the old bias, hatred and contempt against Jewish Christians. In doing so they are guilty of misleading their people, and of discrediting their true brethren and most worthy friends. As Isaiah wrote,"O my people, they which lead thee cause thee to err, and destroy the way of thy paths" (Isa. 3:12). Christ Himself referred to such people as "blind leaders of the blind."

Sometimes Jewish expressions of censure and condemnation of Hebrew Christians are extreme: "It is only a worthless, ignorant and mentally feeble Jew who is ensnared by missionaries or so-called Christian friends"; or, "a convert is a knave, a low-down creature who sells his soul for money or other material gain." Or again, such judges insist, "the Jewish people have lost nothing, have not become poorer, by the defection of such Jews, and we say 'Good riddance.'" A rabbi scornfully commented concerning those who become Christians: "What falls off is offal!"

But such is the confusion and superficiality of Jewish thought in this respect that these same critics complain that "most converts are of the upper classes of Jewry, men of wealth, of talent and of genius, whose loss to Jewry is irreparable!" Accordingly, they seek by all means at their disposal to prevent the conversion of Jews to Christianity. In addition, Jewish converts are frequently accused by their critics of turning against their own people and of being connected with anti-Semites in maligning and harming their fellow Jews.

It is, therefore, part of the purpose of this book to refute such faulty assertions and flimsy accusations. The biographies show that it is emphatically not true that only unworthy Jews accept Christ. It will be obvious to all readers that Jews who accept

Christ do not become enemies of their people, and do not entertain condemnatory or unworthy thoughts about them.[2]

Indeed, Hebrew Christians exemplify and declare that Christ cares about every human being whether they be rich or poor, strong or weak, high or low, ignorant or learned. The most cultured, scholarly, and upright need and may receive His compassion and salvation. The worst sinners and most depraved criminals, even unsatisfactory Jews, may come to Him confidently to find forgiveness and peace. His sacrifice was for all—for each and every human being, without exception. Jesus Himself declared: "Him that cometh to me I will in no wise cast out" (John 6:37). And the apostle Paul gives the same assurance: "For whosoever shall call upon the name of the Lord shall be saved" (Rom 10:13). By such an act of coming or calling the convert, be he Jew or Gentile, is admitted to a new life in God wherein he is "created in Christ Jesus unto good works which God hath before ordained that we should walk in them." All converts are expected to be practicing Christians, not merely passive believers. The Christian life is a life of faith *and* works.

The eminent Jewish Christians described in this book have been selected to refute the view expressed by some Jewish leaders that only the lowest type of Jew is likely to believe in Christ and to accept Christian doctrines. Even in the time of Christ, Jewish leaders mockingly asked, "Have any of the rulers or of the Pharisees believed on him?" (John 7:48).[3] They refused to acknowledge that any learned Jew would be found among the multitudes that followed Christ. Only the *Am-ha-Aretz*, the

2. Benjamin Disraeli (who became Lord Beaconsfield) never sought to hide his Jewish origin. By name and appearance he was typically, and obviously, Jewish. In some of his public speeches he spoke openly and with pride of his Jewish descent (see pp. 70–74).

3. The number and eminence of the Jews who believed in Jesus as Messiah and Savior supplies a valid answer to the question posed by the chief priest in John 7:48. The New Testament clearly and convincingly records that many eminent men among the Jewish people believed on Him—most of them openly, but some secretly. Also, individuals described in this volume came from homes where the Torah was loved, honored, faithfully observed, and devoutly studied. Several were being trained and taught with a view to their becoming rabbis. Some were, indeed, rabbis at the time of their conversion. Relatively few were ignorant of the Torah or simply rejected it (see John 5:46–47; Luke 24:27; John 1:45). The observant Jew has but to "search the Scriptures" (the Law and the Prophets) to find Messiah Jesus set forth as He appears in the New Testament record, the mediator of the New Covenant (see Jer. 31:30 and Isa. 53).

unlearned and ignorant masses, could be so gullible as to believe the "impostor" Jesus. Outstanding Jewish believers have been purposefully presented here to disprove such unfounded assertions.

If a Jewish convert leaves his natural environment and associates, even his family, it is not because he has deserted them, but because his fellow Jews and friends have rejected him. He would much prefer to remain a Jew among Jews than be compelled to move into a totally foreign environment. Nevertheless, his love for his own people, and his loyalty to them remains. It is, indeed, stronger upon conversion. Many Hebrew Christians are inspired by this greater love to seek the salvation and blessing of their people.

Some Jews charge that the Jewish missionary is a "soul snatcher." Rather, his object is to lead his fellow Jews into a fulfilled, fuller, and happier life in Christ. He does not, as some Jews actually assert, receive a cash bonus for every Jew he leads to Christ. A missionary's salary is meager and inadequate by commercial and professional standards, so he must make great financial sacrifices and forego many comforts in his service for Christ and his own people. In addition to these deprivations he frequently has to endure scorn and suffering visited upon him by his fellow Jews, even by his own family.

Contrary to the foolish claim of some skeptics, the Jewish convert does not expect or receive any payment or reward when he becomes a Christian. Often, in fact, he suffers real material loss. Indeed, no financial bonus could ever adequately compensate the convert for the lasting pain imposed by the loss of parents, kinsfolk, friends, and associates (sometimes even the loss of employment), home comforts, and the "surgery" of being cast out of his natural background and environment. Nothing in the non-Jewish world can replace these things. Happily, he does find comfort, love, and hope in his Redeemer Christ, who sustains and satisfies him in every part of his being.

Obviously it is utterly mistaken to charge that the only Jews who become Christians are cowards and cannot sustain the consequences of their Jewishness in an unfriendly world. Plainly, the step of faith in Christ calls for courage and self-sacrifice of a very high order. These things being so, Jewry has ample reason to be proud of the outstanding Jewish men who have become Christians, and have endured the opprobrium and ostracism imposed on them.

It must be remembered that it was the early Jewish followers of Christ who initiated and sustained the spread into all the world of "the good news of God concerning his son Jesus Christ," the gospel of Christ, which is "the power of God unto salvation to every one that believeth; to the Jew first . . ." (Rom. 1:16).

That so great a number of eminent and worthy Jews were confident of the validity and relevance of their faith in Jesus Christ should prompt serious and impartial consideration of their convictions and claims. Rejection of these claims (and the claimants) is often due to sheer, overbearing ignorance, and a denial of soundly-based genuine experience. Their faith in Christ is "faith that bringeth salvation." The critic, therefore, should examine his prejudices and his premises, and soliloquize: "Were these converts perhaps right? Should I not therefore think seriously about the welfare, salvation, and peace of my people, and of my own soul, and of the relation of Jesus Christ to these things?"

The answer to such an important inquiry is to be found in the Jewish Scriptures of the Old and New Testaments, in the life and work of Jesus Christ, and in the reality of Christian experience, particularly Hebrew Christian experience.

Introduction

There are many Christians who, while they accept and commend Christ's command to "preach the gospel to every creature," are nevertheless doubtful about the need and the propriety of preaching the same gospel to the Jews. But the various reasons propounded for this exclusion of the Jews all do violence to the comprehensiveness and clarity of the missionary mandate. They are contrary to the teaching of Scripture and the universal purpose of God's grace: "God . . . now commandeth all men every where to repent" (Acts 17:30).

Failure to preach the gospel to Jews is nothing less than a missionary "blind spot." Justification for it is sometimes sought in the feeble argument that missionary witness among the Jews "does not pay." Some even say that "with the money spent for the conversion of one Jew, ten or more Gentiles could be converted." But human souls must never be measured in monetary terms; to adopt such an attitude is to risk falling into David's sin of counting heads (I Chron. 21).

Results depend on the will and grace of God who, through the operation of His Spirit, alone can give the increase. Christ did not commission His disciples to be evangelistic statisticians but to preach the gospel. Similarly, the Old Testament prophets were commanded of God to prophesy, even when it was certain that the people would not hear or obey them. See, for example, Ezekiel 2:5, "And they, whether they will hear, or whether they will forbear, (for they are a rebellious house,) yet shall know that there hath been a prophet among them" (cf. also Ezek. 3:17–21; I Cor. 1:17).

Another objection raised against the evangelization of the Jews is that "since the Jews have rejected Christ, He has rejected them." Though most Christians admit that any Jew may still accept Christ and join the Christian fellowship, many feel there is no necessity or obligation to specially persuade the Jews.

This, of course, is invalid. After His rejection by the Jewish leaders, His cruel death at the hands of Roman soldiers, and His triumphant resurrection, Jesus commanded His disciples to "preach the gospel to every creature," beginning at Jerusalem, that is, "to the Jew first." That was both His first and His final post-resurrection command. Paul both preached and gave practical demonstration of his faith "to the Jew first," though he was "the apostle of the Gentiles."

The record and the declaration of God's Word ought never to be forgotten or lost sight of, for God's covenant with and mercy toward the Jewish people are everlasting (Gen. 17:7; cf. Jer. 31:3, 35–36). Not until the whole universe disintegrates and disappears can God's love and care for Israel cease. Theological hair-splitting and ill-founded speculations cannot change the plain and permanent truth of Holy Writ.

Why God chose the descendants of Abraham as the agents and instruments for the unfolding and effectiveness of His plan of salvation for mankind; why He revealed Himself to them primarily and progressively; why He sent His prophets to them (and only to them); and why He sent to them His only begotten Son, belongs to the counsel of His own will. "How unsearchable are his judgments, and his ways past finding out!" (Rom. 11:33). Even Paul pondered this awe-ful mystery (Rom. 9), but until God ultimately makes things plain, this matter must remain a mystery. Even so, it is a facet of divine truth and requires acceptance and acquiescence. In fact, it might justifiably be argued that if God had not chosen "stiff-necked" Jews like Paul and set them apart as His messengers to communicate the gospel to every creature—by preaching it "to the Jew first"—

possibly no creature, Jew or Gentile, would have come to Christ.

Indeed, the civilized world of Paul's day, the Roman Empire, was steeped in crude paganism on the one hand, and in Greek secularism on the other. It was inconceivable that the sophisticated, proud, pleasure-loving, and powerful Romans should renounce their popular idols, their intellectual presuppositions, and their philosophy of life to accept instead the religion of a persecuted minority Jewish sect—a religion which subordinates life in this world to some mystical world to come, and which even most Jews rejected. If Paul and his fellow apostles had been subject to the limited practical considerations which restrain so many present-day Christians, they might not have undertaken the seemingly unpromising task of preaching the gospel to the Gentiles. For in its earliest days, Christianity was looked upon as a Jewish sect; it was an apparently hopeless task to convert a Gentile into a "Jew" of the Christian persuasion. But Paul and his fellow apostles were constrained to "preach Christ crucified" to the Jews to whom it was "a stumbling-block," and to the Greeks to whom it was "foolishness" (see I Cor. 1:18–25).

Jesus, however, confined His earthly ministry to the Jews ("I am not sent but unto the lost sheep of the house of Israel," Matt. 15:24.) Many thousands of Jews believed and followed Christ in response to His words and His work. Following Christ's crucifixion and glorious ascension Peter remained in Jerusalem. As a result of his preaching at Pentecost and thereafter, thousands of Jews received Christ as Messiah and Savior, and the Book of Acts is the historical and factual record of this. The general apostolic labors resulted in many thousands of conversions among the Jews. That the number who became believers was very great is evident from Acts 21:20. Here the Greek word "murias" is used, and means literally "a myriad," or ten thousand, although it is probable that the writer's intention was simply to denote "many thousands" (see Acts 2:41–47; 4:4; 5:14). Further testimony to the phenomenal increase in the number of believers is given in Acts 6:7.

Thus, and obviously, the church in Jerusalem was composed entirely of Jews. And Jews became, necessarily, the first missionaries of the Christian church by preaching among the Gentiles "the unsearchable riches of Christ." The bishops of Jerusalem from the Apostolic Age to about A.D. 132 were Jews, as were also some of the outstanding leaders of the church in Gentle lands. Of these bishops of Jerusalem, Eusebius, "the father of ecclesiastical history" (d. A.D. 340), writes:

> The chronology of the bishops of Jerusalem I nowhere found in writing, for tradition says that they were all short-lived. But I have learned this much from writing, that until the siege of the Jews, which took place under Adrian, there were fifteen bishops in succession there, all of whom were said to have been of Hebrew descent, and to have received the knowledge of Christ in purity, so that they were approved by those who were able to judge of such matters, and were deemed of the episcopate. For the whole Church consisted then of believing Hebrews who continued from the days of the apostles until the siege which took place at this time; in which siege the Jews, having again rebelled against the Romans, were conquered after severe battles. But since the bishops were of the circumcision at this time, it is proper to give a list of their names from the beginning. The first then was James, the so-called brother of the Lord; the second Simeon; the third Justus; the fourth Zacchaeus; the fifth Tobias; the sixth Benjamin; the seventh John; the eighth Matthias; the ninth Philip; the tenth Seneca; the eleventh Justus; the twelfth Levi; the thirteenth Ephres; the fourteenth Joseph; the fifteenth Judas. These are the bishops of Jerusalem that lived between the age of the apostles and the time referred to, all of them belonging to the "circumcision."

When, under the emperor Constantine, the church became the state religion of Rome, it lost much of its purity and power, and became significantly paganized and corrupt under an unworthy political ecclesiasticism. It did, however, increase in numbers.

In the Middle Ages the church entered a new "Dark Age," and was divided by severe and damaging conflicts. This period was especially disastrous for the Jews. To them the church appeared as a new idolatry of menacing and brutal forces to be distrusted and shunned. The Jews rejected the church, with its brutalities and blandishments.

With the rise of Protestantism and the Reformation, the darkness of corruption and error which discredited and weakened the church was to a great extent dissipated. Many Jews have since glimpsed something of the "eternal light" of the true Christian faith, and a significant number have thereby found a haven of rest and safety in Christ.

In the course of time, the rise of evangelical Christianity led to the emancipation of the Jews in many lands, and presented the opportunity of escape from the life of the ghetto and freedom from its evil influence on Jewish mental and spiritual life. But many preferred the spiritual bondage inherited from their fathers, and resisted all outside influences. On the other hand, some were eager to acquaint themselves with the life and the ideas of the Christian world about them. And there were those who read the New Testament seriously and searchingly, for since the Reformation the New Testament had become available for all to read. Through it many Jews came to the knowledge of Christ.

There are no reliable statistics of the number of Jews who confessed Christ and joined the church in the years immediately following the Reformation, but there are records from the nineteenth century. In 1899 the Rev. J. F. de le Roi, a missionary of the London Society for Promoting Christianity Among the Jews, published his book, *Jewish Baptisms in the Nineteenth Century*, which recorded that 224,000 Jews were baptized in that period.

According to *The Universal Jewish Encyclopedia* (1941), "these figures are manifestly too low.... Actually the number of converts during this period must have been considerably higher." Under the heading *Converts*, the encyclopedia lists about two hundred eminent Jews of the nineteenth century who converted to Christianity. The list is, however, extremely limited. It does not include those whom it calls "apostates," that is to say, those converts who, according to the encyclopedia's definition, have manifested animosity towards Jews and Judaism, or have attempted to persuade other Jews to become Christians. Unfortunately, there have been a few converts who for some reason were hostile to their fellow Jews or to Judaism. They were simply unnatural or de-natured Jews. For no true Christian, Jew or Gentile, can hate or be hostile to other human beings.[1]

The Jewish list cited mentions the Hebrew Christian humorist, Moritz Gottlieb Saphir (1795–1858), but makes no

---

1. Certainly missionaries to the Jews cannot be charged with despising or denigrating their fellow Jews. I have personally known hundreds of Jewish missionaries and have never met one who hated his own people. Rather, the Hebrew Christian missionary preaches and exemplifies to his fellow Jews the gospel of love and salvation, and that out of a strong and sincere love for his people.

reference to Adolph Saphir, the missionary, though Israel never had a greater friend. The list also excludes many Hebrew Christians who attained international fame in various fields, although they were not ostentatiously Christian. For instance, the outstanding astronomers Sir Frederick William Herschel (1738–1822) and Sir John Frederick Herschel (1792–1871), are omitted. (Perhaps the omission was an attempt to avoid confusion with one of the greatest Jewish missionaries, the Rev. Ridley Haymin Herschell, founder of the British Society for the Propagation of the Gospel among the Jews [1842]).

The composition of this list categorically refutes the charge that only poorer, uneducated Jews became Christians. Indeed, it names more than two hundred Jewish Christians who received the highest recognition in the most notable fields of human endeavor. These eminent Hebrew Christians brought honor to their people, for many were staunch defenders of the honor, rights, and integrity of the Jewish people.

Of the 224,000 Jewish converts referred to by the Rev. J. F. de le Roi, 72,000 were baptized into Protestant churches. This represents approximately one Protestant convert to every 156 Jews of the then Jewish world population. The number of baptized converts from among the Moslem and other non-Christian populations in the same period was about 2,000,000. Had there been the same degree of effectiveness among non-Jews as among the Jews, there would have been something like 7,000,000 converts instead of 2,000,000. Such figures totally refute the claim that "with the money spent for the conversion of one Jew, ten or more Gentiles could be converted."

The August 17, 1883 issue of the British *Church Times* said of Jewish converts: "There is reason to believe that there is no family of the human race which, on the whole and in proportion to its size, yielded more converts to Christianity." There is certainly no less truth in the claim now. Many Jewish converts are, however, absorbed and merged into the Christian community, and numerical estimates are not so easily arrived at. Moreover, it is more than likely that the children of such converts have readily accepted and adapted to the Christian environment.

Some time before World War II, the veteran Hebrew Christian, Elias Newman, estimated that of the then world Jewish population—about 16,000,000—there were probably at least half a million Jews who professed faith in Christ. Add to this number the descendants of former converts, and the number of both true and nominal Christians of Jewish origin would reach a generous seven-figure total.

According to Rev. Newman, more than three times as many Jewish converts entered the Christian ministry as did converts of other non-Christian groups. At that time there were about 1,700 Jewish Christian ministers. Six hundred Lutheran clergymen in Germany were of Jewish descent, which was three percent of the Protestant ministry of that country.[2] In the United States of America there were then about 25,000 Hebrew Christian members of evangelical churches, nearly four hundred of whom were ordained ministers. There were also many thousands of Jewish members of non-evangelical churches. According to Dr. Louis Meyer, statistician of the *Encyclopedia of Missions*, 83 percent of Jewish converts were the direct result of missionary activity. What other mission field has produced such a record of converts? It is a portrait gallery of men of faith and fervor who can take their stand with the heroes of faith set forth in the eleventh chapter of Hebrews. They were men from every walk of life, who represent all areas of human achievement.

We must emphasize that Jewish Christians who have been active as clergymen, church officials, and theological scholars have brought credit, dignity, and blessing to the Christian church, as have also the many Jewish laymen whose lives and labor have been a powerful testimony to dynamic of the gospel of Christ.

We must also mention the great "cloud of witnesses," those unknown Hebrew Christians who remained inconspicuous and undistinguished, possessing no special talents, performing no outstanding function or service in the church. These all lived and died in faith, and contributed the richness of their faith and faithfulness to the general good of the church. Many bequeathed to the church the heritage of godly and great sons and daughters whose quality and achievements have graced the church and its witness. For example, General Booth, the founder of the Salvation Army, was born of Hebrew Christian stock.

---

2. During the Nazi genocidal onslaught against the Jews of Europe, Jewish converts numbering nearly one and a quarter million suffered the same fate as did non-Christian Jews. Most of these were slaughtered by the Nazis or met death through the horrors of the concentration camps.

Thus, the results of Christian witness and missionary testimony to the Jews are manifest, momentous, and meritorious. The means expended and the manpower employed are completely and convincingly justified. The brief biographical sketches in this book which follow afford clear proof of this to both Jews and Gentiles. Jewry may be justly proud of her Christian sons and daughters. And the church universal has ample cause to honor those Jewish men who, through Christian witness and missionary work, have gone forward by the grace of God, from Judaism into "the liberty wherewith Christ makes free."

It should here be mentioned, however, that the following biographies omit such nominal Hebrew Christians as Heinrich Heine, Fritz Haber, Emim Pasha, and Gustave Mahler, who contributed little to the church and its mission. Also omitted are those Jews who upon conversion joined the Roman Catholic or Greek Catholic churches. These number many hundreds, and some of the Jewish converts reached high eminence in the Catholic hierarchy by becoming archbishops, bishops, cardinals, and so on. Despite the ceremonial practices and doctrinal extremes of these churches, the intellectual and spiritual gifts of these Jewish ecclesiastics have, in many instances, greatly enriched the Christian church as a whole.[3]

Obviously, limitations of space prevent the inclusion of many Jewish Christians who have worthily contributed to the growth and glory of the Church. The names of present-day Hebrew Christians have also been omitted, for selection would have been difficult. There are so many important individuals that a comprehensive study would require a far larger volume, or even further volumes, simply to refer briefly to each prominent contemporary Hebrew Christian bearing his or her witness around the world. Suffice it to say that Hebrew Christians are legion, and are to be found in all walks of life.

Hebrew Christians have always been among the most tena-

---

3. Some writers have said that the Reformation might not have occurred without the influence of Hebrew Christians. During the time of Martin Luther some even claimed: "Si Lyra non ligrasset, Luther non saltasset"; "If Lyra had not played the strings, Luther would not have danced." Nicholas of Lyra was a fourteenth-century Hebrew convert, and a great biblical scholar and writer. His commentary on Romans influenced Luther in his grasp of the doctrine of justification by faith. John Wycliffe, the English philosopher and reformer, was also influenced by Lyra.

cious defenders of "the faith which was once delivered to the saints." In the earliest days of the church, Jerusalem and Antioch were the centers of theological thought and development. Most religious thinkers in those cities literally accepted and interpreted the Scriptures and the gospel as originally proclaimed by Jesus and His apostles. Jewish converts were at the forefront in the refutation of Gnosticism, with its non-literal, spiritualizing treatment of Scripture which obscured the true meaning of the Word.

In the nineteenth century, when agnosticism spread through Europe and the United States, largely through the dogma of liberal clergymen and ministers, Jewish Christians rose to the defense of Christian truth as taught in the Word of God. Among such protagonists were August Neander, Alfred Edersheim, Isaac da Costa and Carl Paul Caspari. Hebrew Christians were also outstanding figures in the propagation of the gospel and the spread of the true faith. For example, Joseph Schereschewsky served as a missionary to China; Solomon Ginsburg was a pioneer missionary in Brazil; Henry Stern went to Abyssinia; Dr. Betelheim pioneered the gospel in Japan, and Isidor Lowenthal took the message to Afghanistan.

Thus, it has been shown that the Jews are not in any way, or for any cause, excluded from the universal intention and comprehensive purpose of the gospel and Christ's commission. Indeed, as we have seen, the Jewish people are especially entitled to receive the blessings of the gospel of Christ. This is no vain claim. Note the apostle Paul's answer to his rhetorical question, What advantage has the Jew? "Much in every way: chiefly, because that unto them were committed the oracles of God." (Romans 3:2). Further, in Romans 9:4–5, Paul speaks of the sevenfold privileges of Israel: "To [Israel] pertaineth the adoption, and the glory, and the covenants, and the giving of the law, and the service of God, and the promises; Whose are the fathers, and of whom as concerning the flesh Christ came, who is over all, God blessed for ever. Amen."

Missionary, Bishop of
Jerusalem
1799–1845

Michael Solomon Alexander

MICHAEL SOLOMON ALEXANDER was born in May, 1799, in
Schonlanke, a small town in Posen, at that time a province of
Prussia. His parents were strict Orthodox Jews, and he was
educated with a view to his becoming a rabbi and teacher of
Judaism. When he was only sixteen, he was known and esteemed for his profound Hebrew erudition and his ability as a
teacher. But he grew dissatisfied with life in the small Prussian
town and its limited prospects, so in 1820 he decided to go to
England. There he hoped to become a teacher of Hebrew and to
perform the rites of a *schohet* (slaughterer of poultry and cattle
for kosher meat). He failed to obtain a suitable situation in
London, and so he accepted a post as tutor in Colchester.

One day while walking in the street he was given a handbill
announcing a local meeting of the London Jews' Society. At
that time he knew extremely little about Jesus and His teachings. Like most Jews of that time, he viewed with hatred and
fear the Gentile "idolatry" known as Christianity, which had so
cruelly persecuted the Jewish people since Jesus "deserted the
Jewish faith and became its adversary." But the handbill
aroused Alexander's curiosity, and he decided to attend the

meeting. There he was given a New Testament, which he secretly and carefully read. He learned that Jesus and His teachings were altogether different from the ideas and opinions impressed upon him since early childhood.

After reflecting deeply upon the New Testament presentation of Christ, he critically examined the opinions of his Jewish teachers. In his search for the truth he asked himself, "Could the rabbis be mistaken, or do they have reason to conceal the truth about Jesus?" These and other such questions urgently demanded valid answers, and he could not dismiss them from his mind.

During this unsettled period he was offered the position of rabbi at Norwich, England, and accepted the appointment. Some months later he took up a similar post in Plymouth where, in 1821, he married Miss Levy. In his spare time, Alexander gave Hebrew instruction to several clergymen, including the Rev. B. B. Golding, curate of Stonehouse. Their frequent discussions led Alexander to consider the possibility that Jesus was indeed the Messiah for whose advent and intervention the Jews had hoped and prayed for many, many centuries. Secretly he visited the church, and, in the shadow of its walls, listened spellbound to the songs of praise being sung within. His growing conviction that Jesus was the Messiah gave rise to inner turmoil. His strong leanings to Christianity soon became clear to his Jewish associates, however, and he was suspended from his rabbinical duties.

This suspension left him free to think and act according to his convictions, and he began attending Rev. Golding's meetings regularly. Eventually, he was firmly convinced of the Messiahship of Jesus. He asked to be baptized, and in this way openly confessed his faith on June 22, 1825, in St. Andrew's Church, Plymouth, England. His wife, unknown to him, had also been a secret inquirer, and she was baptized six months later. Alexander then followed a course of Christian theological training. In 1827 he was ordained deacon in Dublin, Ireland, and was appointed to a small charge there. That same year he was ordained priest by the bishop of Kildare. He joined the London Jews' Society, serving as missionary in Danzig, Poland, from 1827 to 1830, and in London, England from 1830 to 1841.

The Jewish people had in him a faithful, courageous defender. During the infamous Damascus "blood accusation," Alexander's name appeared at the top of a long list of names of

Jewish converts who subscribed to a formal "protest of Jewish Christians in England." These converts were protesting the slanderous accusation that Jews used Christian blood in their Passover rites. The fact that these Jews had reached maturity in the faith and practice of Judaism before they became Christians gave special significance to this remarkable document.

In his work in London, Alexander frequently preached to groups of Jews. He took an active part in the revision of the New Testament in Hebrew, and in the translation of the liturgy into Hebrew. He also held the post of Professor of Hebrew and Rabbinical Literature in King's College, London, from 1832 to 1841.

In 1841, King Frederic William IV of Prussia desired to ameliorate the condition of Protestants in the Holy Land, and to secure for them equal privileges with the Greek, Latin, and other churches. Taking advantage of the reestablishment of the Turkish suzerainty by the aid of Christian Europe, the king proposed to the British government that a united effort be made to place a bishop in the Holy City as the Protestant representative. This proposal was heartily welcomed, and the British Parliament passed a bill to establish and endow such a bishopric. The bill received the royal assent on October 5, 1841. (The Anglican bishop was to be nominated alternately by the crowns of England and Prussia, but it so happened that England appointed a bishop twice and Germany only once. After the withdrawal of the Germans in 1887, the bishopric of Jerusalem became an exclusively Anglican bishopric.

The bishopric was first offered to the Rev. Dr. McCaul, but McCaul recommended that the episcopate of St. James ought to be held by a descendant of Abraham. It thus came about that the most conspicuous Hebrew Christian in England was selected: Michael Solomon Alexander.

Alexander's consecration as the first bishop of the new See took place on Sunday, November 7, 1841 in Lambeth Palace. The act of consecration was performed by the Archbishop of Canterbury, Dr. Howley, assisted by the bishops of London, Rochester, and New Zealand, in the presence of a distinguished company. Among the dignitaries were representatives of the king of Prussia, and the British Ambassador Extraordinary to the Porte (the court of the Turkish sultan in Constantinople). Dr. McCaul preached the consecration sermon from Isaiah 52:7, "How beautiful upon the mountains are the feet of him that bringeth good tidings, that publisheth peace; that bringeth good tidings of good, that publisheth salvation; that saith unto Zion, Thy God reigneth!" On the following morning, Holy Communion was celebrated in the Episcopal Jews' Chapel by the new bishop; in the evening Alexander preached his last sermon before leaving England to take up his new post. His text was Acts 20:22–24,

> And now, behold, I go bound in the spirit unto Jerusalem, not knowing the things that shall befall me there: Save that the Holy Ghost witnesseth in every city, saying that bonds and afflictions abide me. But none of these things move me, neither count I my life dear unto myself, so that I might finish my course with joy, and the ministry, which I have received of the Lord Jesus, to testify the gospel of the grace of God.

Subsequent events gave these words a prophetic significance.

On December 7, Bishop Alexander and his wife; his private chaplain, the Rev. G. Williams; the Rev. and Mrs. F. C. Ewald; and Dr. E. MacGowan sailed from Portsmouth in the steam frigate *Devastation*, granted for the purpose by the British government.

The entry of the bishop into Jerusalem was a unique event in the history of the Holy City, and he himself described it as follows:

> On Friday evening we arrived in the city of our forefathers under circumstances of peculiar respect and honour.... We formed quite a large body—the Consul General Colonel Rose, with seven or eight of his escort; Captain Gordon and six of seven officers of the *Devastation*; Mr. Nicolayson and Mr. Bergheim, who met us at Jaffa and accompanied us; Mr. Johns and the American missionaries with escorts, who came to meet us about three miles from Jerusalem; and, at last, the chief officers sent by the Pasha who had himself come to meet us in the afternoon but was obliged to return as night came on and it was damp; and a troop of soldiers headed by Arab music, which is something like beating on a tin kettle. Thus we entered through the Jaffa Gate, under the firing of salutes, etc. into Jerusalem, and were conducted to Mr. Nicolayson's house where we were mostly kindly and hospitably received. All felt overwhelmed with gratitude and adoration. We had service in the temporary chapel on Sunday last. I preached my first sermon from Isaiah 60:15....[1]

1. Quoted in *Jewish Intelligence*, 1842, p. 127.

The London *Times* contained a full account of the bishop's arrival and concluded that "the Mission is sure of the firm support of the British government and the British ambassador at the Porte. Concerning Syria, the Consul-General has lent all the force of his official authority, personal influence and popularity, to set the undertaking afloat, while the mild and benevolent character of the bishop, and the sound practical sense and valuable local experience of the coadjutor, Mr. Nicolayson, are sure guarantees that caution, charity and conciliation will preside at all their efforts." In conformity with orders received from the government in Constantinople, proclamation was made in the mosques that "he who touches the Anglican Bishop will be regarded as touching the apple of the Pasha's eye."

In his first letter, dated February 2, 1842, the bishop referred to revival of the work. Speaking of the daily services in the temporary chapel, he wrote, "I feel it peculiarly delightful thus daily to worship on Mount Zion." He was greatly encouraged that many Jews showed interest in the progress of the new buildings. The bishop had frequent conversation with them. A second letter, dated March 9, stated: "Our mission is beginning to be very interesting and, I trust, efficient. There never have been such large congregations of Protestants as have been assembled since my arrival here. On Sunday last our chapel was literally crowded, and never did I wish more than our church was built. I will have laid the first foundation stone on the 28th April.

But the bishop and his assistants had to overcome almost insurmountable difficulties, and not a little antagonism. Much commotion was caused in Jerusalem when three rabbis placed themselves under Christian instruction. Jews all over the country were incensed and exasperated, and they did all in their power to prevent their people from coming into contact with the missionaries. Despite all obstacles, however, the work progressed.

On May 19, 1843, the bishop opened an institution for the training of Hebrew Christian missionaries. In the same year another institution was established for the training of converts in carpentry and joinery. A few years later the institution became a home as well as a workshop—converts and inquirers were housed, maintained, and instructed in the Christian faith while they learned a trade at the same time. The trades of printing and bookbinding were added as part of the curriculum. In 1844, a "Bible depot" was opened for the circulation of the Holy Scriptures in Hebrew, Arabic, Greek, Italian, French, German, and Spanish, and for the distribution of various tracts in Hebrew. This occasioned great alarm among the Jewish leaders, and the threat of excommunication was pronounced by the rabbis against every Jew entering the premises.

On December 12, 1844, a hospital was opened for poor, sick Jews. There was a great deal of opposition on the part of the rabbis, but it gradually became a great blessing to Jews of all classes who readily resorted to the hospital when in need of medical attention and nursing care. In time, the opposition exhausted itself.

On November 26, 1845, Bishop Alexander died, after an episcopate of only four years. He died while traveling in the desert at Ras-el-Wady, on his way to visit Egypt, which was part of the diocese of Jerusalem. Touchingly, in the bishop's last annual letter, written before he started for Cairo, he had joyfully announced that the *firman* (license) had been granted for the erection of the church, and spoke of the progress of the work. His wife described those last days in the desert as follows:

> On setting out through the desert each day my beloved husband and myself rode our own horses; we generally were in advance of the caravan, and we used regularly to chant some of our Hebrew chants, and sang . . . hymns. Never did his warm and tender heart overflow so fully as when he spoke of Israel's future restoration. When I spoke to him about his duties in England he answered, "I hope, if invited, to preach my first sermon in England at the Episcopal Jews' Chapel," and on my asking what subject he would take he replied, "I shall resume the subject I adopted when I last left that dear congregation," namely, that none of these trials had moved him—Acts 20:24–28.

The immediate cause of death was the rupture of one of the large blood vessels near the heart; but the lungs, liver, and heart were all discovered to be diseased and had been so for some time. The accelerating cause was, no doubt, the great and continued anxiety that the bishopric of Jerusalem and its cares produced. As one of his traveling companions commented, "Had his lordship not come into the East, he might possibly have lived to a good old age; but the mitre of Jerusalem, like the wreath of our blessed Lord, has been to him a crown of thorns."

A letter of condolence to Mrs. Alexander, signed by thirty-one Jewish converts at Jerusalem, is a most eloquent testimony to the blessings which the bishop's labors had brought:

> We feel collectively and individually that we have lost not only a true father in Christ, but also a loving brother and a most kind friend. . . . The affectionate love he bore to Israel, which peculiarly characterized him, could not fail to render him beloved by every one who had the privilege of being acquainted with him: while his exalted piety, and the most exemplary life and conversation, inspired the highest reverential esteem. He was a burning and a shining light; and when he was raised to the highest dignity in the church, he conferred the most conspicuous honor on our whole nation, but especially on the little band of Jewish believers. With him captive, Judah's brightest earthly star has set, and the top stone has been taken away from the rising Hebrew Church.[2]

Many friends testified of their love and esteem for the bishop by raising £3,000, which was given to his widow and family. The list of contributors reveals that the bishop was highly esteemed by rich and poor alike. Among the names are Queen Adelaide; the archbishops of Canterbury and Armagh; the bishops of London, Winchester, Ripon, Lichfield, Lincoln, Peterborough, Llandaff, Sodar and Man, and Madras. The Primate of All England stated that Alexander conducted the affairs of his church with so much discretion and prudence that he gave no cause for complaint to the heads of other communions residing in the same city. He won their esteem by his piety, beneficence, and by his perserving yet temperate zeal in pursuing the objects of his mission.

Alexander lived and worked in constant dependence upon the Holy Spirit, whose power he conspicuously honored. He impressed upon those whom he instructed the impossibility of their understanding divine things without the Holy Spirit's aid. This was as noticeable in his earlier years as missionary as in his later ones as bishop. His conciliatory manner in dealing with Jews, his love for his brethren, and his calmness amid opposition did much to appease the excited assemblies at the conferences in Aldermanbury, and the violent attitude of the mob when he revisited his Jewish relatives at Schonlanke. He

2. Quoted in *Jewish Intelligence*, 1846, p. 128.

was bold and fearless in the delivery of his message, faithful in everything, anxious about all things to bear testimony to the name and glory of his Master, and to make full proof of his ministry, whether as missionary or as bishop.

His friends, and those who worked under him at Jerusalem, loved him for his kind nature (for he had an ear, heart, and purse open to all) and for his simple-hearted piety. He was indeed an Israelite in whom there was no guile. He had a ripeness of Christian experience, and unaffected earnestness of purpose. He was a strikingly interesting personality, rendered doubly so in that he was a Hebrew of the Hebrews, and in his Episcopal dignity a link with the primitive Hebrew Christian church in the mother city of Christendom.[3]

3. The account of Alexander's death is taken from *The History of the London Society for Promoting Christianity Among the Jews*, by the Rev. W. T. Gidney.

2

Writer, Evangelist,
Missionary
1855–1926

David Baron

DAVID BARON was born at Suwalki, Poland, in 1855, and his upbringing and training were under strict rabbinical guidance and influence. When he was only four he was taken to *cheder* (Jewish religious school), and within six months he was able to read Hebrew. After two and a half years in the local school his father brought him to an uncle in a neighboring town for instruction in the Talmud, but a year later he had to return home because of illness.

Two months later, his father placed him under the care of a local rabbi. Shortly afterward he had a serious accident; he was hit by a horse-drawn cart. He was severely injured, taken home unconscious, and the doctor gave no hope for recovery. In four weeks, however, he was up and about again. His father engaged a private tutor to instruct him in the Russian and Polish languages.

At the age of ten, Baron entered the Yeshivah, the rabbinical college, where he soon became one of the most outstanding and proficient students. Eighteen months after beginning his studies there, he gained first prize for distinguished scholarship. At his bar mitzvah ceremony he delivered a Talmudic discourse which won him great praise and commendation.

A few years later, one of his brothers-in-law decided to emigrate to American, and it was decided that Baron should accompany him. During their journey through Berlin the brother-in-law's money was stolen, and Baron gave him most of his own so that the brother-in-law could continue his journey to America. Baron used what little money he had left to travel to England. His destination was the Yorkshire town of Hull, where he hoped to earn enough to enable him to follow his brother-in-law to the United States. For a while he was alone and friendless, and when his father learned of his plight he sent money and advised him to return home. But Baron had made up his mind to remain and make his own way. His religious education, inclinations, and instinct amply equipped him for an individual and independent approach to life.

In addition to his strength of character and keenness of intellect, Baron was a man of deep spiritual experience. Very early in life he was profoundly conscious of the oppressive burden of original sin, and he often pondered the question, How can a man be just before God? He carefully studied the various passages in the Torah and other parts of the Old Testament which tell of the the corruption and sinfulness of man, such as Genesis 6:5 and 8:21; Psalm 60:5–7; and Jeremiah 17:9.

He earnestly endeavored with heart and mind to be a good Jew, and to please God. He diligently studied the Talmud, and carefully observed the laws and rites prescribed by the rabbis. But in the depths of his soul he felt that his good works and religious observances were not sufficiently meritorious in the sight of God. He perceived God as an all-powerful tyrant, watchful and condemnatory, who observed human beings— and especially Jews—to note whether they diligently kept His laws and to inflict severe punishment upon the least transgression of His will.

David Baron was deeply distressed when he thought on the inescapable pronouncement of Deuteronomy 27:26—"Cursed be he that confirmeth not all the words of this law to do them," and the declaration of Ezekiel 18:20—"The soul that sinneth, it shall die." Eagerly Baron searched the Scriptures to find some assurance of the forgiveness of sins. He was arrested by these words: "It is the blood that maketh an atonement for the soul"

(Lev. 17:11). This led him to a deeper study of the sacrifices which occupied such a large part in the temple worship at Jerusalem. Through his studies he saw that most Jewish prayers revolve around the invocation seeking a return to Zion and the reestablishment of the ancient sacrifices.

After he was injured by the horse-drawn cart, Baron was greatly distressed lest he should die and go to hell. His mother tried to reassure him that he was a good Jewish boy, and that if he died he would go to paradise. But his mother's words brought him little comfort, for David Baron felt that being good was not sufficient in the light of Isaiah 64:6—"We are all as an unclean thing, and all our righteousnesses are as filthy rags. . . ."

During his search, his mind laid hold on the revelation of Isaiah 53 which told of "the man that bore our sins," but the passage puzzled him. One of his commentaries referred the passage to the Messiah, but he dismissed the idea as absurd. He had been taught from childhood that the Messiah would be a great king and a mighty hero who would save the Jewish people from their enemies, and would restore their kingdom and make them supreme over all nations. Nothing had been communicated to him about the Messiah's power to redeem men, both Jew and Gentile, from sin.

In England David Baron first heard this transforming message of the Messiah who died to make atonement for the sins of mankind, and to bring salvation to individual men and women. In April, 1877, during his early days in Hull, a Hebrew Christian missionary, Mr. Koenig, invited Baron to attend his Saturday gospel meeting. He accepted the invitation and went to the meeting, intending to assail the missionary with arguments refuting his claims. Like most Jews, he despised Jewish missionaries, and felt that his questions would quickly confound the speaker. But what he heard compelled him to keep silent and to deeply reflect to see whether the testimonies and teaching he had listened to were indeed true. Mr. Koenig gave him a New Testament, which he took to his lodging and began to study.

As with all Jewish children of his time, Baron had been indoctrinated against Christ. He had been taught that Jesus was a seducer turning Jews away from God; his teachers had insisted that Jesus was an imposter who had been condemned to death for his wickedness and blasphemy. In the New Testament,

Baron discovered the real Jesus Christ, a glorious personality in whom dwelt all the treasures of wisdom and knowledge. But it was not easy for Baron to break with his past or to escape from the weight of his Jewish religious teaching and tradition. For six months he passed through a period of deep spiritual distress and uncertainty, and earnestly searched the Scriptures, comparing the teachings of the Old and the New Testaments.

During this time of spiritual travail, David Baron came to London to consult with the Rev. John Wilkinson, the well-known missionary, and Mr. James Adler, both of whom he had met at the Hull mission. After a month of more concentrated inquiry, he at last found a true spiritual relief and rest for his soul in the blessed assurance of complete salvation in Christ. On October 17, 1878, David Baron was baptized by sprinkling by Rev. Wilkinson, and was later baptized by immersion by Dr. C. Y. Biss.

At once Baron wrote to his father telling of his conversion, and assuring him that he had not deserted his Jewish people, nor the God of Abraham, Isaac, and Jacob, the God of the Jews. But his explanations did not mollify his father nor modify his father's opinion, the opinion held by every Jew, that any Jew who embraces Christianity is an apostate, a renegade, and a traitor. And, according to Jewish custom, his father observed seven days of mourning for his "dead" son. (A few years later, however, Baron succeeded in persuading his father that he truly believed in the God of Israel as revealed in the Bible and in Israel's history, and there was a reconciliation of sorts.)

In 1879, Rev. Wilkinson sent Baron to Harley House College with other believing Jews for Bible and missionary training. Finishing his course in July, 1881, he joined the missionary staff of the Mildmay Mission to the Jews. For two years he worked among the Jews in Scotland, and at the end of that time returned to London. His connection with the Mildmay Mission to the Jews lasted for twelve years. His work was in London, and he also made missionary journeys abroad. He never identified himself with a particular branch of the Christian church, for he considered the many divisions of the church as a serious stumblingblock to the Jews. His sole aim was to present to his fellow Jews the Lord Jesus Christ, in all His majesty, grace, glory, and virtue, as their true and only Messiah. In this Baron sought unremittingly to offer clear and consistent proof from

Holy Scripture that Jesus is "the way, the truth, and the life" to Jew and Gentile alike.

From 1885 to 1889 David Baron and a Mr. Barnett, a fellow worker at the Mildmay Mission, were engaged in preaching the gospel to Jewish communities along the Russian frontier and in Germany, Austria, Hungary, Galicia, and Bohemia. In the spring of 1890, David Baron and Dr. Dixon were sent on a missionary tour to the East, and in 1891 Baron and Barnett were appointed to work in Palestine.

The major development in Baron's career as a missionary to the Jews came in 1893. In that year he and Charles Schonberger, (see chap. 29), brother-in-law of Dr. Adolph Saphir, (chap. 27), founded the Jewish mission known as The Hebrew Christian Testimony to Israel. Baron and Schonberger first met in 1887 in Europe, where Schonberger was working with the British Society for the Propagation of the Gospel Among the Jews. In this new venture for God, and for the missionary cause among the Jews, Baron and Schonberger detached themselves from the missions with which they had been associated for many years. Without in any sense questioning the aims and methods of others, they united on lines which they felt were more in harmony with the requirements of the Jewish mission field. In their new enterprise they did not operate as representatives of any group or sect, or with a view to converting Jews to a particular creed. As they themselves had in Christ found the Messiah of Israel, so they wished to bear their testimony to as many of their own brethren as possible, and to lead them into a redemptive relationship with Christ.

Throughout his mission and ministry, David Baron never himself administered baptism to converts. If a converted Jew asked for baptism he was advised to get into touch with a Baptist chapel whose minister was known to be sound in doctrine and of fundamentalist outlook. When asked why he refrained from baptizing converts Baron referred his questioner to I Corinthians 1:17—"Christ sent me not to baptize, but to preach the gospel."

These missionary colleagues had no guaranteed salary or regular income and found it difficult to make ends meet. For the first two years they had no house or center for their mission. They were content to be itinerant missionaries and evangelists, speaking to Jews wherever they could reach them, both at home and abroad. The work of the "Testimony" began in a room in the West End of London, loaned for that purpose for one or two nights a week. Later a somewhat dilapidated house in London's East End Jewish quarter in Whitechapel Road was rented, which served as a center for about six years. This house was, however, both unsatisfactory and unsuitable, and the fetid atmosphere of overcrowded and ill-ventilated rooms was a danger to health.

The work continued to grow, and on January 31, 1901, the present mission house was opened. Fifteen years later adjoining premises were acquired to meet the increasing demands of the work. (Unfortunately, both houses were severely damaged by bombs during the 1940–41 air attacks on London, but they were completely repaired and restored.) The work was, throughout, wholly maintained by the free-will offerings of the Lord's people, and Baron received nothing from mission funds for his own support or use.

One very important factor in the widespread influence of the Hebrew Christian Testimony to Israel was its literature produced for Jewish readers. The Testimony published thirty-eight books and many pamphlets in several languages from Baron's pen. He was a prolific writer of books and tracts which were circulated among the Jews in almost all the lands of their dispersion. Baron, who thus distinguished himself as a writer, traveler, missionary, preacher, and evangelist, much preferred to be known simply as a missionary to his own people. He maintained that it was his chief joy and privilege "to lead these poor Jews, often sunk into such lamentable ignorance of the precious Book of God which is the foundation of all our blessedness in Christ, into the light of the Word of Truth."

In his closing years, ill health prevented him from continuing his active part in the work of the mission. His frequent absences from the mission house caused him great sorrow. Although illness afflicted him over a long period, his love for his people and for the mission was so intense that, contrary to the advice of his doctor, he labored ceaselessly and unsparingly to the end. On October 22, 1926, he became seriously ill, and pneumonia developed. He had so spent himself in the service of Christ and Israel that his powers of resistance and recuperation were diminished. On October 28, at the age of 71, he was taken to be with Christ. The following tribute of fellow missionaries reveals the impact of Baron's life and teaching:

It was not to his own people alone that Mr. Baron confined his attention; he devoted a large share of his time and effort to the church of Christ. . . . He found that the characteristic weakness of present-day Christianity is superficiality and shallowness. He searched to discover the main cause of this, and came to the conclusion that "it is chiefly to the . . . fragmentary, vague, disjointed, textual manner in which the Bible is being dealt with that the lamentable lack of depth and backbone in Christianity today is due. It is also owing chiefly to this cause, and to the neglect or misinterpretation of typology and prophecy, and the ignoring of the position of Israel in relation to the purpose of God as revealed in the Scriptures, that the Old Testament has become 'as the words of a book that is sealed' to the majority of professing Christians." He therefore decided to "unfold . . . whole Scriptures, and thus let the sacred oracles speak for themselves."

Mr. Baron's life, preaching, and personality were an inspiration. His teaching through his books indicates not only his well-stored mind, but his intense veneration for the Scriptures as the Word of the Living God, and his implicit faith in their divine origin from beginning to end. . . . No one can fail to see the Bible was the daily food of his soul, his teacher and counselor, his trust and his treasure.

3

*Bible Scholar
and Linguist
1804–1886*

Joachim Heinrich Raphael Biesenthal

RAPHAEL, so named by his parents at his circumcision, was born on December 24, 1804, in Lobsens, a small town in the then Prussian district of Posen. His pious parents intended that he grow up to be a Jewish scholar and rabbi. To this end they did all they could to ensure his instruction by the best teachers available, first of all in his home town. Later he was sent to study at the Yeshivoth (Talmudic academies) of Posen and Rawitsch, and finally at Mainz, where he acquired an extensive knowledge of Talmudic literature, the Bible, and other Hebrew writings. Privately he learned German, Latin, and Greek, and quickly became proficient in these languages.

In 1827 he went to Berlin, where he earned his living by teaching, and used his leisure time for private study and attendance at lectures in the university. For four weeks in 1830 he lived with a Christian family. Their piety made such a deep impression on him that he decided "to search for Christian truth." Being so determined, he got in touch with several Christian pastors. In 1835 he studied theology and philology at the University of Berlin, where he was awarded his Doctor's degree.

The following year he was baptized, and took the names Joachim Heinrich and the surname Biesenthal.

Dr. Biesenthal revealed the details of his spiritual journey eight years after his baptism, when he offered himself as a missionary candidate to the London Society for Promoting Christianity Among the Jews. In his letter of application he wrote:

> My Biblical studies led me, after much searching and wandering . . . , to find Him of whom "Moses in the Law, and the Prophets did write." This result, this light which God caused to shine in my darkness, I deem it my unrelenting duty to communicate to others yet living in darkness, because the Lord Himself says that we should not put our light under a bushel. The apostles, as well as the Fathers, were furthered by the same disposition of mind. "For where your treasure is there will your heart be also," says the Lord. If Christ be our treasure, our heart must be entirely and undividedly His own, and all our talents devoted to the glory of His kingdom. Becoming a missionary seems to me to be the surest way to fulfill Christ's commands.
>
> I have long considered it both a duty and a privilege to communicate to my brethren after the flesh the message of salvation, and to employ those talents which God has given me for their welfare. My predilection for the above has often seemed to be a token of God's will that I should show my brethren from their very literature, as well as from the Bible, that the treasures of wisdom and knowledge are hid in Christ, and that we can only know the Father through Him. During the last three years I have acted upon this conviction, and embraced every opportunity to prove to my brethren that the Gospel of Christ is the power of God unto salvation, and my anxious desire now is to be enabled to devote all my time to this pursuit.

His missionary service with the society covered a period of thirty-seven years, and this time was spent in Berlin from 1844 to 1868, and Leipzig from 1868 to 1881. In his missionary work among all types and classes of Jews, his extensive knowledge of biblical and rabbinical literature was an invaluable and effective asset.

In addition, his linguistic abilities constituted a true "gift of tongues" that included Hebrew, Polish, German, French, English, Spanish, Italian, Arabic, Latin, Greek, Syriac, Chaldee, Ethiopic, and Syrian. He was also gifted with his pen in promulgating the knowledge of Christ among the Jews. In Germany his name was for many years a household word because of his scholarship; and his commentaries on the Gospels, the Epistle to the Romans, and the Epistle to the Hebrews were established works of reference in mission work. While he was in Berlin he edited the society's monthly periodical, *Records of Israel's State and Prospects*, and wrote many articles for the *Dibre-Emeth*, and several other Christian publications.

Dr. Biesenthal's ministry in Leipzig was of even greater importance, since the city was a center of trade. Jewish merchants from various parts of Europe and from distant countries visited the great fairs held in the city, and there were excellent opportunities to present the good tidings of Jesus. Dr. Biesenthal's work not only produced direct, observable results in the form of baptisms, but his ministry also had important and far-reaching indirect effects.

But during that period there came dark and frustrating days for Jewish mission work. In Germany, the spread of socialism and rationalism, which gained a firm hold in universities and churches, attracted and influenced many Jews. At the same time anti-Semitism burst forth with great virulence, and the Jews met hatred with hatred. Zeal for mission work died out. In such a situation, and in such circumstances, Dr. Biesenthal found it almost impossible to engage in direct mission work, and devoted his time to literary activities. Franz Delitzsch, the noted Hebraist and translator of the New Testament into Hebrew, called Dr. Biesenthal's commentaries the best writings ever issued in aid of the cause of Jewish missions.

Among Dr. Biesenthal's published works were: *Auszuge aus dem Buche Sohar, mit Deutscher Uebersetzung* (1837), a proof from Jewish sources of the doctrine of the Trinity and other Christian verities; *Hebraisches und Chaldaisches Schulworterbuch uber das A. T.* (1836–37); *David Kimchi's Liber Radicum* (1838–48), in collaboration with F. S. Lebrecht; *The Thirty-nine Articles of the Church of England* (1840); *The Book of Psalms, Hebrew Text and Commentary* (1841); *Chrestomathia Rabbinica Sive Lidre Quatuor* (1844); *Menachem ben Serug's Hebrew Lexicon* (1847); *Theologisch-Historisch Studien* (1847); *Zur Geschichte der Christlichen Kirche* (1850); *Das Trostschreiben des Apostels Paulus an die Hebraer* (1878); and a Hebrew translation of the Epistles to the Hebrews and the Romans, with commentary (1857–58). In addition, Dr. Biesenthal wrote commentaries on the Gospel of Matthew and the Book of Acts, an essay on the atonement, and a biography called *The Life of Gerson*. Dr. Biesenthal also wrote, under a pseudonym, a book defending the Jews against the Damascus "blood accusation" (see pp. 30–31). In his *History of the Christian Church,* written especially for Jews, he set forth how essentially Jewish the early church was, and that it was Jewish believers in Christ who effectively labored for the spread of the gospel in those first years of missionary enterprise. Dr. Biesenthal's literary genius attracted widespread attention, and eminent Jewish authors such as Dr. Isaac Jost, the great historian, and Dr. Julius Furst, gave high praise to his valuable contributions to Hebrew as well as Christian Literature.

In 1877 Dr. Biesenthal received the Doctor of Divinity degree from the University of Gliessen. Three years later he retired from missionary work and, in order to be near his eldest son, a physician, returned with his wife to Berlin, where he died on June 25, 1886, at the age of 82.

4

Physician and
Author
1795–1874

Abraham Capadose

ABRAHAM CAPADOSE'S life and conversion is one of the
most interesting and inspiring chapters in the history of Jewish
mission work.[1] Abraham Capadose was born in Amsterdam in
1795, the son of a prominent and prosperous Portuguese Jew. He
enjoyed a close and happy relationship with his cousin Isaac da
Costa (see chap. 8) and moved in the same wealthy and influential circles.

Although his busy life as a physician claimed much of his
time and energy, Capadose was able to give himself diligently
to a purposeful examination of the claims and teaching of
Christianity. In his inquiries he was much impressed and influenced by Justin Martyr's *Dialogue with Tripho the Jew*, as well
as by the fifty-third chapter of the Book of Isaiah. In this respect
Dr. Capadose's experience was similar to that of a great number
of Jewish inquirers who have read and reflected upon the
prophet's inspired "report" concerning Israel's Messiah, given

---

1. It is not possible to include all the details of this remarkable Hebrew
Christian's experience in a brief biography. What follows in this biographical
sketch is derived mainly from the autobiography Capadose sent to his friend
Ridley Herschell in London.

seven hundred years before His advent. And like many, he was convinced of its authenticity. His response is typical, and expressive of the convictions of many Jews who have found the Messiah:

> One night I was reading in the prophet Isaiah; on arriving at the fifty-third chapter, I was so much struck with what I read, and clearly perceived in it, line for line, what I had read in the Gospel about the sufferings of Christ, that I really thought I had got another Bible instead of my own. I could not persuade myself that this fifty-third chapter, which may so well be called an abstract of the Gospel, was to be found in the Old Testament. After so reading it, how was it possible for an Israelite to doubt that Christ was the promised Messiah?
>
> Whence could so strong an impression have come? I had often read that chapter, but this time I read it in the light of God's Spirit. From that moment I fully recognized in Christ the promised Messiah, and now our meditations on the Word of God assumed quite a new character. [In using the first person plural Capadose refers to da Costa and himself.] It was as it were the beginning, the dawn of a magnificent day for our souls; the light shed more and more upon us of its enlivening influence; it enlightened our minds, warmed our hearts, and even then gave unspeakable comfort.
>
> I began to perceive the reasons of the enigmas so often occurring in life, and which, till then, had occupied me rather in the way of fatiguing and distressing, than of tranquilizing and instructing me. All things around me seemed to live anew, and the object and interest of my existence underwent total change. Happy days, blessed by the consciousness of the Master's presence! . . .
>
> I can seldom peruse the account of the two disciples going to Emmaus, without recalling those days on which my friend [da Costa] and I used to meet and walk together. Like the disciples we can say: "Did not our heart burn within us, while he talked with us by the way, and while he opened to us the scriptures?" (Luke 24:32.) It was then that the rays of the Sun of Righteousness, which dawned upon us, shed upon us not only a light that illuminated, but that life-giving and celestial warmth also, which made us live the life of God.
>
> I saw that love had led the Saviour to seek me; I began also to feel my sins, or rather, let me say, my total misery. But this sentiment was absorbed, as it were, in a sense of the divine love. I had experienced it; I had found my life in Christ; He became the central point of all my affections and of all my thoughts, the only object capable of filling the immense void in my heart, the key of all mysteries, the principle of all true philosophy, the truth—the truth itself.[2]

2. Quoted from *The Conversion of Dr. Capadose*, pp. 13–15.

Although Capadose was by birth a Portuguese Israelite, before his conversion he was by no means zealous of the religion of his fathers. His education was moral rather than religious. At an early age he was captivated by science and literature. He was fond of balls, plays, and every worldly amusement; but study afforded him still greater satisfaction. He became acquainted with the works of Voltaire and Rousseau at an early age. However, because he saw the consequences of their systems exhibited in the history of the French revolution, he was preserved, by divine mercy, from their influence. His parents desired that he enter the medical profession, and so he considered it his duty to acquire knowledge requisite for this calling. He felt, however, more inclination for the study of the theoretical sciences and for philosophic research.

Most of his friends were young men who outwardly professed Christianity; except for his cousin, Isaac da Costa. Because they were both Israelites, and had been intimate from childhood, their views on many subjects were similar. They both at this time had a friendly association with the notable Christian and outstanding Dutch poet Willem Bilderdijk (whom da Costa considered a major influence in his own spiritual pilgrimage).

Of his attitude toward Judaism, Capadose writes:

> At the synagogue, which, for the sake of decorum, I still frequented, nothing had the least power to interest me. On the contrary, the unmeaning ceremonies which appealed not to the heart, the want of reverence, the bawling noise, the discordant singing, and lastly, the employment of a language of which three-fourths of the congregation did not understand a word, disgusted me so much, that I ceased to attend it regularly, having always a great aversion to hypocrisy.

In 1818, he took his degrees in medicine, left the university, and returned to his native Amsterdam, full of bright prospects for the future. He had an uncle there, one of the best physicians in Holland, a learned man, and highly esteemed by the principal families. Having no children he took Capadose into his house and adopted him as son and successor. Capadose was thus introduced at once to an extensive circle of acquaintance; kind and respectable, but with whom Christianity was a mere outward profession accompanied by an entirely worldly life. None of these ever spoke to him on the subject of Christianity. He even heard some of his young friends make a boast of their infidelity, and speak without reverence of the Lord Jesus Christ. Capadose writes:

> I once expressed my astonishment at this, and said, that though I did not believe in Jesus, I thought that those who worshiped Him, and did not consider Him to be God, were mere idolaters. A young physician who was of the party, who was afterwards savingly converted to God, told me some years after, how much ashamed he felt at the time, when receiving such a reproof from an Israelite.

Dr. Capadose goes on to tell of his dejection because of his spiritual conflict. His inner struggle so deeply depressed him that he wrote he wished he could die. But after much study of the Scriptures he became convinced that in Christ was all his life, his thought, and his affections, "the sole object that could fill the void in my heart; the key of all mysteries; the principle of all true philosophy, yea the truth itself."

> When the change became known to my family, they first used gentle means with me, in the hope that these new notions might pass away; but finding I grew bold, and ventured to preach the Gospel to them, they resorted to harsh treatment. It was a season of deep trial to my soul. This state of things increased the ardent desire I felt publicly to confess Christ. My family wished me to go into Germany, or some other country, for this purpose; but to this I objected, lest it should appear as if I were ashamed of the step I was about to take. My friend da Costa and I at length decided on Leyden as the place where we would receive the rite of baptism. The 20th of October, 1822, was the day so ardently desired, on which we were admitted members of the Church of Christ. Kneeling in the presence of the congregation, before the God of our fathers, who is the true God—Father, Son, and Holy Spirit—we had the unspeakable joy, unworthy sinners as we were, to confess before the Christian Church, the blessed name of that great God and Saviour, who had come to seek and save us when we were lost. Glory be to God.

Among Dr. Capadose's writings the most noteworthy are: *Aan mijne geloofsgenooten in de Ned., Heb., Gem.* (The Hague, 1843); *Overdenkingen over Israel's Roeping en Toekomst* (Amsterdam, 1843); and *Rome en Jerusalem* (Utrecht, 1851).

Dr. Capadose died on December 16, 1874, at the age of 79, and triumphantly entered the presence of the Lord he had served so well and so long.

5

*Theologian,
Missionary
1814–1892*

Carl Paul
Caspari

THE GERMAN TOWN of Dessau, capital of the free state of
Anhalt, was made famous in Jewish history by its connection
with Moses Mendelssohn, the great Jewish philosopher. He
was the spiritual father of the Jewish movement of modern
culture and enlightenment, and the grandfather of Felix Mendelssohn, the famous composer.

It was in Dessau that Carl Paul Caspari was born in 1814, the
child of enlightened and devoted Jewish parents. In Dessau
there was a modern Jewish educational institution, and preaching in the synagogue was in the German language instead of
Yiddish, an unusual and generally unacceptable innovation at
that time. Religious instruction was also given from the modern
viewpoint, and the interpretation and approach was profoundly influential in molding the character and outlook of
young Caspari.

When only twenty years of age he left Dessau for Leipzig in
order to study Oriental languages at the university. There he
became acquainted with the New Testament, through his friend
and former schoolmate, Charles Granel. Granel, who later became the President of the Missionary Society of Saxony, en-

couraged Caspari to study the New Testament seriously. At first Caspari's interest was somewhat casual and cursory, but he quickly became intrigued by the Lucan account in Acts of the persecution of Paul by the Jews. Feeling that what he had read was historical truth, he decided to read the New Testament from beginning to end.

The record of the life and work of Jesus, as presented in the Gospels, made an immediate and indelible impression upon Caspari's heart and mind. His reading strongly persuaded him that this gentle, loving, and compassionate Jesus might help him in the perplexities that troubled his soul and mind. When, long afterward, he spoke of this experience, Caspari said: "I came to Him as to my only Savior, just as in the days of His flesh others came to Him and found refuge."

But Caspari had still to overcome stern inner struggles before making his final decision. In this time of spiritual and intellectual travail he was greatly helped by his friend Granel, by Joseph Wolff of Leipzig, (see chap. 33), and by Professor Franz Delitzsch. (Delitzsch, who translated the New Testament into Hebrew, was a great friend of the Jewish people; it was from him that the Institutum Judaicum Delitzschianum in Munster took its name.) Through the help of Granel, Wolff, and Delitzsch, Caspari's search and struggle for the truth were climaxed in the victory of saving faith. He was baptized on Easter Sunday, 1838, by Pastor Zehme, who had also baptized Professor Friedrick Adolph Philippi, the outstanding Hebrew Christian who bore a prominent witness in the Lutheran Church (see chap. 23).

After his baptism Caspari turned his attention to theology, and especially to the study of the Old Testament. He wrote a commentary on Obadiah, and an Arabic grammar which became a standard work and appeared in many languages.

Some time after the completion of his university course, he received a call to the university of Konigsberg. He declined the invitation, however, for he wished to work only in a Lutheran institution. The opportunity to do so came in 1847, when he received an invitation to the University of Christiana in Norway. Here Caspari was soon recognized as an outstanding theologian and a champion of true Scriptural faith. He wrote expositions of many Old Testament books, and gave important help in editing the newly revised Bible in the Norwegian language. His research concerning the Apostles' Creed, which at that time agitated the northern evangelical churches, was considered to be significant and decisive.

Caspari's conversion and his many labors for Christ did not, however, alienate him from his Jewish brethren. His love for them grew with his faith, and he never ceased to pray for them and for their salvation.

In 1865 Caspari was appointed president of the Norwegian Central Committee for Jewish Missions, and he later became director of the Lutheran Central Societies at Leipzig. He also served zealously and devotedly in connection with the Students' Missionary Association at Christiana. His lecture to the Society in 1891 on Jewish missions is of special importance. In that lecture he discussed four major questions:

1. *Is Jewish mission work necessary?*
   Yes! Without it the majority of Jews would never be reached by the preaching of the Gospel.
2. *How shall Jews be converted?*
   By in every church establishing societies of earnest Christians who shall support proselytes from Judaism as missionaries among their own people.
3. *How shall these missionaries carry on their work?*
   Not by dispute and argument, which create only intellectual knowledge, but through the promulgation of the way of salvation, must the Jews be encouraged to embrace the truths of Christianity, through which Christians also are converted.
4. *How are the converts to be treated?*
   They might primarily be organized into circles, to serve as leaven among their friends (much, of course, depends upon their various former environments).

Caspari was certain of Israel's glorious place in the unfolding of God's purpose. To a great extent this governed his missionary thinking, and his loving zeal for the salvation of his Jewish brethren. In 1891 he had the great pleasure of ordaining the first Norwegian Jewish missionary.

To the dismay and sadness of his many friends, Caspari's work among them ceased in 1892, when he was "called home" at the age of 78. He had fought a good fight, he had finished his course. His work was done, but what he had begun was continued by others. He was eulogized as one of the most eminent witnesses for Christ, and was numbered among the outstanding defenders of Scripture truth during the nineteenth century. Professor Bang referred to him as "the teacher of all Scandinavia," and testified that his death was regarded as a very sad event in the history of the church. Pastor J. F. de le Roi wrote of him: "His own great aim in life was to be found ever trusting simply in the mercy of Christ; and the rock to which he clung in his dying hour was the word of the Savior: 'Him that cometh unto me I will in no wise cast out.'"

Some of Professor Caspari's works are: *Commentar uber Obadja* (Leipzig, 1842); *Beitrage zur Einleitung in das Buch Jesaia; Untersuchungen uber den Syrisch Ephraimitischen Krieg unter Jotham und Ahas* (Christiana, 1849): *Commentar zu Micha* (Christiana, 1852); *Theile des Jesaia seit 1853; Zur Einfuhrung in das Buch Daniel* (Leipzig, 1869): *Quellen der Geschichte des Taufsymbols und der Glaubensregel* (Christiana, 1868–69); *Grammatica Arabica* (Leipzig, 1842–48, a second edition appeared in 1866).

6

Missionary
1821–1893

Selig Paulus Cassel

THAT SO OUTSTANDING a Jew as Paulus Cassel should become a Christian is a testimony to the truth and power of the gospel, and a challenge to the reserve and animosity of non-Christian Jews. Cassel was a star of the first magnitude in the galaxy of great Jews who became convinced and steadfast Christians. Even among those Jews who disparagingly call Jewish Christians *meshumadim*, "renegades and traitors," there have been those who held Cassel in high regard. Thirteen years before he died (in 1893), the *Jewish Chronicle*, one of the foremost Jewish publications, wrote of him: "A genius like Cassel is always an honor to his former brethren in the faith."[1]

Cassel was born in Glogau, Silesia, on February 27, 1821. His parents made sure that he received a comprehensive and complete education. He was not only brought up to be learned in Jewish lore and life, but was also sent to public school to acquire a good secular education. There he came under the influence of Christian teachers. Once, during the Christmas season the headmaster told his pupils to learn the Christmas

1. *Jewish Chronicle*, January 9, 1880.

57

story. As a Jew the young Cassel was not required to carry out
that exercise, but he did so. He recited the story in class with
such feeling that his delighted teacher kissed him. The fact that
a Christian should kiss a Jewish boy made a very deep and
lasting impression on Cassel and its emotional effect remained
with him all his life.

Indeed, this deep emotional experience might well have been
one of the early impressions leading to his conversion some
years later. At the age of thirty-four, after much study and en-
quiry, Cassel realized and laid hold on the veracity of Jesus'
claims to be the Messiah of Israel and the Redeemer of the
world.

Cassel was, in fact, an outstanding student, had a brilliant
academic career at the University of Berlin, and went on to
establish a reputation as a man of letters. He received many
academic and university honors for his valuable contributions
to learning and literature. His literary and intellectual abilities
were widely acknowledged, and were publicly honored when
the German Prime Minister appointed him editor of the
Deutsche Reform.

For a brief period Cassel took an active part in politics and
became a member of the Prussian Parliament. However, because his editorial and parliamentary responsibilities interfered with his studies, he relinquished both positions after a
short time in office. But while he was in Parliament he was able
frequently to defend his fellow Jews against the virulent attacks
of A. Stoecker, a fellow Parliamentarian and notorious anti-
Semite. Cassel's courageous public defense of the Jewish
people brought him a significant degree of popularity among
the Jews. Both the Jews and the Christians recognized that his
adoption of the Christian faith was not prompted by any ulterior motive. From the moment of his conversion he became a
zealous missionary, for he longed earnestly that his Jewish
brethren might share the joy and peace he had found in Christ.
His missionary zeal soon became widely known, and when the
Church Mission to the Jews built its church in Berlin in 1846,
Cassel was appointed missionary-in-charge. The church had a
spacious sanctuary, capable of containing a congregation of at
least a thousand. It was regularly filled with worshipers, both
Jews and Christians, who were attracted by the quality and
power of Cassel's teaching.

Writing of this period in his missionary work and in his ministry, Cassel states:

The special blessing of the church consisted in the regular exposition of the Old Testament. It has been my custom to expound the Old Testament every Sunday evening, from the first Sunday I came into office up to the present time. It was the first time in Berlin that this was made a practice. There were, therefore, from the very beginning, hearers consisting of Jews and earnest Christians. Those expository sermons have been the greatest blessing and have specially united me to the congregation.

Jews of all classes came both to his church and to his home to be instructed in the Christian faith. During his ministry in Berlin he baptized 262 Jews from various walks of life—though most were well-educated people with literary interests and from the learned professions.

Cassel was in continual demand as a speaker in all parts of the country. Because his courageous and reasoned championship of the Jews was so effective and his lectures were so brilliant, many Jewish literary societies invited him to lecture. When invited to lecture to Jewish clubs he insisted that they name the subject, and he faithfully dealt with the theme decided upon. But when he was "in the saddle," as he called it, he always "rode to Calvary" and pointed his listeners to the crucified and risen Christ.

Writing to friends in England in 1887, at the time of the vicious attacks on Jews by the German anti-Semitic movement, he wrote:

During the anti-Semitic agitation, such journeys for the purpose of delivering lectures were most extensive. I had then become known through my defense of gospel charity, even in circles which were not outwardly known as Christian. The meetings which were held at the period resembled more nearly the ideal at which I aimed. A considerable number of people listened to my lectures who had completely turned their backs on the church.

During this period his literary output was immense. His tracts and pamphlets had an enormous circulation. Many Jews were led to Christ by this means, and many more were given a new view of Christ and His teaching. But because of failing health, Dr. Cassel resigned from his ministry at Christchurch in

1891, though he continued to preach and write as often as his physical condition would allow. In 1893, after a full and fruitful life, he passed peacefully into the presence of the Lord he had served so well among both Jews and Christians.

In his book, *Jewish Witnesses for Christ*, the Rev. A. Bernstein writes of Cassel:

> His gigantic intellect, marvelous ability, persuasive oratory, and brilliant pen, were alike consecrated to the service of the Lord and Master, and to the spiritual welfare of his brethren. Sage, philosopher, scholar, author, preacher and missionary, he was a king amongst his fellowmen. His name will live immortal in the annals of Jewish and missionary literature.

And even the Jewish press, though it regretted his departure from the Jewish faith, paid many fine tributes to Dr. Cassel's life, character, and accomplishments.

7

Dutch Poet Laureate
1798–1860

Isaac da Costa

ISAAC DA COSTA came from an illustrious Jewish family. His ancestors, the Marranos, escaped from Portugal in the middle of the fifteenth century. Many Spanish or Portuguese Jews were forced, under the terrors and tortures of the Inquisition, to renounce their Jewish faith and embrace Catholicism. A great number of these, however, secretly adhered to Judaism. Many escaped to other countries, especially to Holland where they were openly welcomed. There was a great exodus of Jews from the countries of their persecution to Holland in 1591, and the city of principal settlement was Amsterdam.

It was in this city, on January 14, 1798, that Isaac da Costa was born. His father was Daniel da Costa, a prosperous merchant. The da Costa family had been connected with the Spanish-Portuguese Synagogue in Amsterdam for about two centuries. In Holland they enjoyed all the privileges accorded by the Dutch authorities to resident Jews.

Daniel da Costa was a man of strict principle and transparent integrity. Because he perceived Isaac's inclination to study, Daniel da Costa destined him to the career of jurisprudence, a pursuit which, though formerly closed to the Jews, had been partially opened to them since the revolution of 1795. Unfortunately, Isaac's physical health did not correspond to his extraordinary intellectual powers and development, and he never knew what it was to feel perfectly well.

From his thirteenth to his fifteenth year he attended Latin classes in Amsterdam, after which he attended a course of lectures in antiquities and literature by Professor Van Lennep. Through these historical lectures, Van Lennep had ample opportunity to assert the authority of the writings of Moses. Van Lennep's lectures clearly vindicated and confirmed the veracity of the ancient records in contrast to the sophisms of Voltaire and other sceptics of the age.

Until that time, da Costa had been troubled by the serious doubts which arose within him. To escape these perplexities he had formed a religious view of his own, a strange, eclectic mixture of various theories and ideas. He was firmly and uncompromisingly convinced of only one thing: the immense superiority of the Jewish people over all other peoples. After hearing and reflecting upon Professor Van Lennep's lectures he was constrained to read the Bible for himself. And, almost against his will, he was powerfully impressed by its clear and compelling truth.

Of that period and experience da Costa wrote:

> The idea of a *positive revelation* was now awakened in my mind; I began to believe in the divinity of the Old Testament and the great truth, gradually developed, was to me a beacon amidst doubt and obscurity. Revealed religion, the divine authority of the Bible, is an historical fact.

Throughout his life da Costa took great pride in his Jewish ancestry, and openly maintained his own Jewish integrity. Indeed, he writes that "in the midst of the contempt and dislike of the world for the name of Jew I have ever gloried in it." His love for his people prompted him to study deeply their history, and particularly their times of prosperity and calamity. He also examined their theology, poetry, and other distinctively Jewish attainments. In this connection he writes:

> Throughout their history, both ancient and modern, I perceived something so extraordinary as to be quite inexplicable, unless we view the Jews as the subjects of remarkable privileges, and of as remarkable downfall; of a special election of God and of an enormous crime on the part of the elect people.

This searching examination of Jewish history and experience prepared him for the recognition and acceptance of the true Judaism which alone is the culmination and fulfillment of the pure divine faith of the Old Testament.

In addition to his accomplishments and reputation in this particular field of study, da Costa gained a name as a gifted and outstanding poet. The Encyclopedia Britannica records that "da Costa ranks first among the poets of Holland." When he was only fifteen, da Costa was introduced to the celebrated Willem Bilderdijk (1756–1831), the greatest of the comtemporary Dutch poets, who was also a great Christian. Bilderdijk believed firmly in the certain fulfillment of the prophecies relating to the glorious future and final conversion of the Jewish people.

Da Costa was strongly drawn to this extraordinary man, and his feelings of attachment and regard so grew that the two became like father and son. Bilderdijk was one to whom da Costa felt he could reveal in fullest confidence his inmost aspirations and thoughts. Their friendship covered a period of eighteen years, until the day of Bilderdijk's death in 1831.

It was Bilderdijk who directed da Costa's attention to the prophecies, and to the promises given to the Jewish people. Under his guidance, da Costa came to realize that all true Christians share the hopes of Israel concerning the glorious reign of Messiah upon the throne of David. Bilderdijk helped da Costa to understand that the ancient Hebrews acknowledged a plurality of Persons in the ineffable unity of God, and that the prophecies of Isaiah 11:53 and 61, Psalm 22:110, and other Old Testament passages were fulfilled in Jesus. As a result, da Costa undertook a close examination and study of the New Testament. The effect of this study was the realization and admission that he "must become the property of Jesus Christ, and must live to Him and by Him," if he was to be a true Christian.

At this time da Costa was greatly influenced by a book written by a Spanish Hebrew Christian, Professor J. J. Heydek, called *Defense of the Faith of Christians*. By it da Costa was convinced that the Jewish and Christian religions were closely linked, but his mind had not yet fully grasped "the truth as it is in Jesus." Da Costa felt that he could recognize only a Messiah who would be a powerful king and who would restore the Kingdom to Israel. The idea of Jesus as a "man of sorrows," whose death must atone for the sins of all mankind, including his, repelled him.

For a time his attention to religious questions was interrupted by the excitement of increasing public recognition. His poems found many admirers, and his other works gained recognition. A further diversion arose from his great love for the beautiful and intellectually gifted woman named Hannah Belmont.

But all these things left "an aching void the world could never fill." Neither popularity, admiration, nor human love could satisfy the longing in his soul for peace and assurance. Such was his unrest that deep depression descended upon him, and he came near to committing suicide. Horrified by what he had almost done, he cried out in desperation and terror: "My God! Forsake me not!" In this extremity of distress there was given to him a vision of the Messiah as set forth in Isaiah 53, which brought him comfort and peace such as he had never known before. But he still remained uncertain and hesitant, unable fully to accept the truth of Jesus the Crucified.

Unable to resolve his doubts, he confided in his Jewish cousin Abraham Capadose, who also belonged to the circle of Bilderdijk's disciples and devotees. Together they began to read the New Testament and examine the truth concerning Jesus. As they searched the Scriptures, they were joined by a third inquirer, Hannah Belmont, whom da Costa would marry in 1821. The three seekers diligently studied the New Testament, and compared its statements and claims with the prophecies of the Old Testament. Soon they were convinced that Jesus was indeed the One of whom "Moses in the Law, and the prophets did write."

Da Costa, however, still shrank from taking the final decisive step of faith, partly out of consideration for his aged father, who might not have survived the shock of his beloved son's conversion. Even after his father's death in 1822, da Costa hesitated, and found it difficult to commit himself to Christianity. Pride was another factor that prevented his making an open confession. To bow in penitence and condemnation before the crucified Jesus seemed to him, the cultured, gifted, and admired poet and author, inconsistent with his qualities and accomplishments.

Finally, however, the Word of God and the Gospel of Christ proved to be "the power of God unto salvation." The grace of

God triumphed over his pride and his hesitancy. He believed! He called upon the name of the Lord, confessed his faith, and he was saved. His torment came to an end and he knew the peace the Savior gives, the "peace that passeth understanding." Added to his own joy of salvation was the joy of knowing that his wife Hannah and his cousin Abraham had also become believers. They were all baptized on October 20, 1822, at Leyden, in the Netherlands.

And da Costa not only found the truth; he lived it and preached it. By his zeal, knowledge, and his love of Christ and for His people, he brought to Christ many members of his family circle, including his mother-in-law. Indeed, he took his place in the ranks of the foremost ambassadors of Christ and champions of His cause.

At that time, the insidious and destructive ideas and claims of rationalism prevailed among all classes in Holland. Da Costa therefore felt it was his responsibility to bear testimony for Christ with tongue and pen at every opportunity, in all areas of ecclesiastical, intellectual, and public life. He never ceased to call his countrymen, and his fellow Jews, to turn to Christ for salvation and peace. He was instrumental in introducing many people to the Bible through the Bible readings he held in his own home, and through his addresses on these occasions which were subsequently published.

In 1823 da Costa published a lengthy pamphlet, *Accusations Against the Spirit of the Century,* exposing and condemning the evils which threatened the country, and calling upon men and women to place Jesus Christ at the center of both personal and public life. The pamphlet had a widespread and productive influence, though many powerful people were, naturally, offended. There was such criticism and opposition on their part that, in spite of da Costa's rare gifts and attainments, these prejudiced and influential political leaders prevented his appointment to any position in the universities or in the service of the government. Despite the opposition, however, it was chiefly due to his influence that Christianity again became a power in the national life of Holland.

This influence was recognized and acknowledged in many quarters. Dr. Joseph Wolff (chap. 33), the prominent missionary and traveler of the London Society for Promoting Christianity Among the Jews, met the Isaac da Costa family in Holland and wrote: "I think that, if I were not yet converted, the wonderful dealing of God with the family of da Costa would strike me with amazement, and might be the means of my conversion." Da Costa's clear testimony and courageous stand won him many friends, not only among the noblest and ablest men in Holland, but also in England, France, Germany, and Switzerland. Like all men of principle and courage, however, he had his opponents and enemies—though even many of these were ultimately reconciled to him. The government itself eventually sought to reward him in recognition of his patriotic writings. This, however, he refused.

His writings continued to extend and consolidate his influence. He produced an interesting and trustworthy contribution to the history of the Jews; the English translation was called *Israel and the Gentiles*. In addition, he wrote several books and pamphlets both of general and of Jewish–Christian interest. After Bilderdijk's death, da Costa was recognized as his successor among the Dutch poets, and he was considered by many the greatest poet his country had produced in the nineteenth century.

But his fervent patriotism and love for his fellow Christians did not diminish his love for his Jewish brethren. To the Christian church he emphasized its duty to Israel—and its debt. To the Jews he proclaimed Jesus as their Messiah. He sought their conversion to Christ by every means in his power. To further this objective he helped to form the Jewish Missionary Society of the Netherlands. And the Jews recognized that da Costa's conversion to Christianity had not alienated him from his race, as a Jew once observed: "You would like to make all the Christians Jews, and all the Jews Christians." Of da Costa the *Jewish Encyclopedia* comments:

> His character, no less than his genius, was respected by his contemporaries. To the end of his life, he felt only reverence and love for his former co-religionists, was deeply interested in their past history, and often took their part.

It is remarkable that one so weak in body and constantly in pain could labor and accomplish so much in the life of the church, in literature, and in both domestic and foreign mission work. During his last illness his pain increased to such a degree that even his physician could not understand how he endured such intense suffering. And so great was his public esteem that bulletins were issued informing the public of his condition. On April 28, 1860, he peacefully and triumphantly gave up his spirit to his Lord. With the words; "There remaineth a rest for the people of God," he died in the arms of his cousin, Abraham Capadose.

8

British Statesman,
Author, Diplomat,
Prime Minister
1804–1881

Benjamin Disraeli
First Earl of
Beaconsfield

AMONG THE OUTSTANDING Jewish Christians of the nineteenth century, none have a greater claim to fame than Benjamin Disraeli. He was a great Jew. He was a great Christian. He was a great politician. He was a great writer. Through his writings, both fictional and political, he championed the cause of his fellow Jews everywhere. His was one of the most astute minds in political history, and no other politician was more devoted to queen and country.

Significantly, the Jews themselves, so often harshly critical and condemnatory of their fellow Jews who become Christians, hold him in high esteem and claim him as one of their own. Indeed, the *Jewish Tribune* of May 7, 1926 records:

Picture what the life and work of this man, though converted
to Christianity, has meant to the Jews languishing under the
yoke of the Czars of Russia and the Kings of Rumania! [Most of
the Jews lived then in these two countries.] Despised and
downtrodden, deprived of almost all human rights, they could
yet point with unfeigned pride to one of their despised brother-
hood holding the reins of government in the great British Kingdom, a man showered with honors and titles of nobility, the
favorite of his Queen, and the equal of the Chancellors of the
great Empires! And that man, moreover, had retained his love for
and pride in his race; acclaimed it from the platform and political hustings, and wrote of it in terms of rapture and longing in
his books! And these books had been translated and assiduously
read by his racial brethren in the dreary ghettoes of Russia and
Poland.

Disraeli never sought to hide his Jewish origins. His name and
facial characteristics were typically Jewish, and he often spoke
with pride in public of his Jewish descent.

He was born in London on December 21, 1804, and died in
the British capital on April 19, 1881. His ancestors were among
the Jews exiled from Spain in 1492, and they settled in Venice.
His grandfather left Venice in 1759 and emigrated to London.
He was the eldest son of Isaac D'Israeli, author of the book
Curiosities of Literature.

For a time Disraeli attended a private school where, when
Christian prayers were recited, he was accustomed to "stand
back"; that is, he was excused from participation. But on July
31, 1817, he, his two brothers, and his sister Sarah were baptized into the Christian faith. This was a few months before his
bar mitzvah should have taken place.

At first Disraeli was destined for the law, but he showed a
decided taste for literature and was allowed to follow his inclination. He tried to make his living, and his fortune, in stocks
and shares, with disastrous results. He failed also in journalism
as coeditor of a daily newspaper with John Murray and James
Lockhard, son-in-law of Sir Walter Scott. But at the age of
twenty-one he produced his first book, *Vivian Grey*, a satirical
novel.

First published anonymously, the novel won immediate and
widespread popularity. It went through three editions, and that
at the time when such great novelists as Scott, Dickens, Thack-
eray, and Kingsley were producing their best work. In later
editions of *Vivian Grey*, Disraeli placed his name on the title

page and thereafter was established as a man of letters. Among his later books were: *The Young Duke* (1831); *Contarini Fleming* (1832); *David Alroi* (1833); *Rise of Iskander* (1834); *Venetia* (1837); *Henrietta Temple* (1837); *Coningsby* (1844); *Sybil* (1845); *Tankred* (1847); *Loathair* (1870); and *Endymion* (1880).

Shortly after publishing his first novel he traveled for some time, visiting Italy, Greece, Turkey, and Syria, gaining experience which he afterwards reproduced in his books. He also visited France, Germany, Spain, Malta, Albania, Egypt, and Palestine. His visit to the Holy Land, and especially to "Jerusalem, the city of a great King," made a deep impression upon him, and inspired within him a vision of the rebirth of Israel. There is some indication he may have wondered whether he himself could be the one through whose initiative his brethren could be gathered once more to their national home, "the Promised Land." This might be assumed from two of his books, influenced by the visit to Palestine: *David Alroi*, the story of a Jewish hero, a pseudo–messiah, who in the year 1117 undertook to deliver Palestine from the Crusaders and rebuild it as a Jewish state; and *Tankred*, which reveals Disraeli's great love for the Holy Land.

Disraeli's political career began shortly after his return from the Palestine visit. With no influential family connection, no noble lineage, no great wealth, and no other advantages, he pressed steadily ahead until he reached the pinnacle of fame and power. After several election contests, some of which he failed, he was elected Member of Parliament in 1837.

Disraeli's early speeches were ridiculed by other members of Parliament, but he told them that the time would come when they would be glad to listen to him! His warning was prophetic. In 1852 and during the years 1858–59 he was leader of the British House of Commons and Chancellor of the Exchequer, a post which he again held in 1866. He was appointed Prime Minister in 1868 and again from 1874 to 1880. This is the highest position in the British government, corresponding to that of president of the United States.

In 1876 Disraeli was named Earl of Beaconsfield, and two years later was plenipotentiary to the historic Berlin Congress. At the congress he won the admiration of the assembled diplomats of Europe. Because of his conduct and influence, Russia was compelled to modify the terms of her treaty with the Turks following the Russo-Turkish War, and Rumania was compelled to grant full religious freedom to the Jews. On his return to England, Disraeli could justly claim to have gained "peace with honor."

Some of Disraeli's actions as Prime Minister greatly changed not only the course of British history but also that of the entire world. Indeed, much of Disraeli's work has since been nullified by the march of events and the effects of two world wars. But had it not been for his actions in diplomacy and debate, all of the Near East might have already passed under total Russian domination. The way for Russia to the African continent and to India would have then been wide open.

Disraeli continued to direct the affairs of the Conservative Party until the time of his death. After he died, the "Primrose League," a large Conservative organization, was formed in his memory. The League commemorates the anniversary of Disraeli's death by holding what is called "Primrose Day." So great was the British people's appreciation of Disraeli and his work that a monument was erected to his memory in Westminster Abbey, Britain's national shrine for its most notable persons.

As a member of Parliament and as Prime Minister, Disraeli was always diligent to ensure justice for the Jewish people. With others, he worked hard and successfully to remove the "disability" against Jews sitting in Parliament. At the Congress of Berlin he made certain that the Jews of Rumania, a severely persecuted minority, were granted equal rights with other citizens.

Whenever he could, Disraeli championed the cause of his Jewish brethren everywhere. His concern for his fellow Jews led his opponents to accuse him of letting his Jewish loyalties dominate his policy in opposition to Russia during the Russo-Turkish War, and later at the Berlin Congress. And his political enemies charged him with too much attachment to and concern for the Jews.

Disraeli not only worked for the advantage of his people as a politician and statesman; he also put forward their cause as an author. In his novel *Coningsby*, the strongest character is a Jew called Sidonia, a wealthy man who speaks eloquently and persuasively in defense of the Jews. *David Alroi* and *Tankred* were among the first novels translated from a foreign language into Hebrew, and they have been read eagerly by Hebrew readers all over the world. Disraeli also spoke for the Jews in his *Life of Lord Bentinck*, where he demonstrated the folly and injustice of holding present-day Jews responsible for the crucifixion of Christ.

But Disraeli never thought it anti-Jewish or un-Jewish to be a Christian. On the contrary, to him Christianity was the true and natural fruition of Judaism. And he asserted Christianity's dependence on Judaism:

> In all church discussions we are apt to forget the second Testament is avowedly only a supplement. Jesus came to complete the "law and the prophets." Christianity is completed Judaism, or it is nothing. Christianity is incomprehensible without Judaism, as Judaism is incomplete without Christianity.
>
> The law was not thundered forth from the Capitolian mount; the divine atonement was not fulfilled upon Mons Sacer. No; the order of our priesthood comes directly from the God of Israel; and the forms and ceremonies of the church are the regulations of His supreme intelligence. Rome indeed boasts that the authenticity of the second Testament depends upon the recognition of her infallibility. The authenticity of the second Testament depends upon its congruity with the first. . . .
>
> When Omnipotence deigned to be incarnate, the Infallible Word did not select a Roman, but a Jewish frame. The prophets were not Romans but Jews; she who was blessed above all women, I never heard she was a Roman maiden. No, I should look to a land more distant than Italy, to a city more sacred even than Rome.
>
> The first preachers of the gospel were Jews, and none else; the historians of the gospel were Jews and none else. No one has ever been permitted to write under the inspiration of the Holy Spirit, except a Jew. For nearly a century no one believed in the good tidings except Jews. They nursed the sacred flame of which they were the consecrated and hereditary depositories.
>
> And when the time was ripe to diffuse the truth among the nations, it was not a senator of Rome or a philosopher of Athens who was personally appointed by our Lord for that office, but a Jew of Tarsus.
>
> And that greater church, great even amidst its terrible corruptions, that has avenged the victory of Titus, and has changed every one of the Olympian temples into altars of the God of Sinai and of Calvary, was founded by another Jew, a Jew of Galilee.

Disraeli expressed a complementary thought in his biography of Lord George Bentinck:

> The pupil of Moses may ask himself, whether all the princes of the house of David have done so much for the Jews as that prince who was crucified on Calvary. Had it not been for Him, the Jews would have been comparatively unknown, or only as a high Oriental caste which had lost its country. Has not He made their

history the most famous in the world? Has not He hung up their laws in every temple? Has He not vindicated all their wrongs? Has not He avenged the victory of Titus and conquered the Caesars? What successes did they anticipate from their Messiah? The wildest dreams of their rabbis have been far exceeded. . . . Christians may continue to persecute Jews (and by so doing misrepresent their Master) and Jews may persist in disbelieving Christians, but who can deny that Jesus of Nazareth, the Incarnate Son of God, is the eternal glory of the Jewish race?

Disraeli anticipated the final conversion of the Jews and expressed the hope that "they will accept the whole of their religion instead of only the half of it, as they gradually grow more familiar with the true history and character of the New Testament."

9

Scholar, Writer,
Theologian
1825–1889

Alfred Edersheim

ALFRED EDERSHEIM was born in Vienna, Austria, on March 7, 1825. His parents were wealthy, cultured people of good social standing. He was their youngest son, and was given the best education enlightened and wealthy Jewish parents could provide. In his early years, Edersheim distinguished himself by his outstanding powers of erudition and oratory. He was held in high regard by Vienna's Jewish community, especially by its youth.

When Adolph Cremieux,[1] head of the French Bar and in 1848 French Minister of Justice, visited Vienna he was welcomed by an address given by Edersheim on behalf of Jewish youth. The address was given when Cremieux attended the synagogue, and Edersheim had been chosen as the young people's representative. Cremieux was so impressed by the young Edersheim's oratory that he desired to take him to Paris under his patronage and provision for life, to train him as a barrister. Edersheim's family, however, would not allow him to go.

1. Adolph Cremieux is known in Jewish history as a staunch defender of the Jewish people, and was the founder and president of the Alliance Israelite Universelle, which has done much for the uplift of diaspora Jewry.

In 1841 Edersheim entered the University of Vienna to study philosophy and medicine. Later, when the family fortunes declined, he supported himself as a student at Budapest, Hungary. While there he studied English under the tutelage of a Jewish medical student named Porgos. As his studies progressed, Porgos had to leave Budapest for six months to undertake a course of study for his doctor's degree. Before leaving he introduced Edersheim to the Rev. Wingate, a Scottish missionary to the Jews, with the request that he would teach Edersheim English and befriend him during his absence.

Rev. Wingate was surprised and asked, "How can you, a Jew, entrust me with your disciple, when you well know that I will have to pray for his conversion?" Pergos replied, "Never mind. I don't know of anybody who could so faithfully care for him during my absence."

In 1842 Rev. Wingate agreed to take Edersheim under his care, and in a very short time Edersheim saw a new light. Wingate's companionship, and that of his associates, greatly impressed and influenced their young charge, so much so that he wrote of that period:

> The purity and holiness of these men attracted me; their earnestness and the firmness of their convictions drove me to investigate their faith, which made them much better than myself or any people I ever knew.... From Wingate I received the New Testament. I shall never forget the first impressions Jesus' Sermon on the Mount made on me, nor the surprise and the profound feeling I experienced while reading the New Testament. The 'Christianity' which I knew as such hitherto was not Christianity. What I did not know was the teaching of Jesus which opened to me such unfathomable depths.

The understanding, affection and prayer of those days provided an environment which, under the influence of the Spirit of God, led Edersheim to faith in the Lord Jesus Christ. In April, 1843, he was baptized by the pastor of the Reformed Church in Budapest.

One of Edersheim's first undertakings in the service of the Lord was the teaching of English to a class of students, with the Bible as the only textbook. Later he decided to go to Edinburgh, Scotland for theological training under the eminent Professor Duncan. Here, and later in Berlin, where he studied under the scholarly and saintly August Neander (see chap. 22), he was thoroughly instructed in theology. On returning to Scotland in 1846 he was ordained to the Presbyterian ministry. Soon afterwards he was appointed to serve the newly organized Free Church of Scotland. He preached in barns, shops, and on the streets. In time those who heard him preach built a splendid church and parsonage. Eventually Edersheim went to Jassy, Rumania, to work under the auspices of the recently established Scottish Mission. Not long after that he was invited to become the minister of the parish of Old Aberdeen, and returned to Scotland. The opportunities for study, and the advantages the university city afforded, were an irresistible attraction.

For the next fifteen years Edersheim diligently studied philosophy and engaged in literary work, combining his studies and his writing with his church duties. These activities, however, imposed a heavy strain on his physical strength and so affected his health that he was compelled to leave Scotland for a warmer climate. He passed the winter of 1860–61 in Torquay, southern England. When he had regained a measure of strength he helped in the founding of a church for Scottish residents and visitors, and served as its minister until 1872, when failing health necessitated his retirement. After resigning his charge he took up residence in Bournemouth, where he wrote *The Temple: Its Ministry and Services at the time of Jesus Christ.*

In 1875 Edersheim became curate of the Priory Church in Christchurch, Hampshire, and published his *Jewish Social Life in the Days of Christ.* Some time later he became vicar of Loders in Dorsetshire. Here he wrote *The Life and Times of Jesus the Messiah,* a book which greatly enriched Christian literature. This book will be a lasting memorial to the rare gifts and unfaltering diligence of the author, and of his utter devotion to Christ.

Edersheim's scholarship was recognized far and wide, and the University of Giessen, Germany, conferred upon him the title of Doctor of Divinity. In 1882 he moved to Oxford where the previous year the university had conferred upon him the degree of Master of Arts. He was later appointed Select Preacher to the university. In 1885 his Warburton Lectures on prophecy and history in relation to the Messiah were published, and in 1886 he was appointed Grinfield Lecturer on the Septuagint at Oxford University.

Among Edersheim's other contributions to sacred literature, the following are worthy of note: *Elisha the Prophet: His Life* and Times; *History of the Jewish Nation from the Destruction of Jerusalem to the Establishment of Christianity in the Roman Empire; Bible History;* and articles for various commentaries and dictionaries. Edersheim was active as translator and editor of various works, and was well-acquainted with Latin, Greek, Hebrew, German, French, Italian, and Hungarian. (His earlier writings included Jewish and German stories translated into English for educational purposes.)

It was Edersheim's intention to publish a companion work to his *Life and Times of Jesus the Messiah* under the title, *The Life and Writings of St. Paul*. He had written the first chapters when his health again failed, and he left home to spend the winter months in Mentone, France. There he seemed to regain his health, and he contemplated the journey home. But on March 16, 1889, at the age of sixty-four, he passed away peacefully to be with Christ.

Edersheim's invaluable contributions to biblical literature are worthy of a fuller account of his life and work. Unfortunately, the sources for such a work are comparatively scanty, due to Edersheim's modesty which restrained him from recording the incidents and experiences of his life. A memoir written by his daughter Ella is a collection of her father's fragmentary thoughts and criticisms. There are also references to Edersheim in Gavin Carlyle's book, *Life and Work of the Late Rev. William Wingate.*

Dean Shailer Mathew of the divinity school of Chicago University, has said that although the *Life and Times of Jesus the Messiah* suffers from an excessive pietism, Edersheim's work is not only "masterly but invaluable. If one were to own but one life of Jesus, it should be Edersheim's" (*The Bible World*, vol. 6, p. 528). Edersheim's *Life of Christ* is a remarkable and outstanding volume. Christendom had failed to produce such an essential and valuable work in the nearly two thousand years of its history. It remained for a Jew to write this book.

Edersheim therefore became one of the world's greatest teachers through the rich and powerful influence of his books. It was his delight to set down and to show how all Jewish hopes were fulfilled in Christ. To the end he remained as intense and brilliant a Jew as he was a profound and faithful Christian.

10

Massoretic Scholar
1821–1914

Christian David Ginsburg

DAVID GINSBURG was born in Warsaw, Poland, on December 25, 1821. At the age of twenty-five he became a Christian, and after due preparation worked in Liverpool, England, as a missionary of the London Society for the Promotion of Christianity Among the Jews. In 1863, when only forty-two years of age, he retired from the mission in order to devote himself entirely to literary work. He had already published editions of the Song of Songs (1857) and Ecclesiastes (1861), and an essay on the Karaites (1862).[1] In the year following his retirement Ginsburg published an essay on the Essenes, and a full account of the Kabbalah, dealing with its development, its doctrines, and its literature. He also contributed various articles on Jewish topics to Kitto's encyclopedia. His greatest work, however, was his Massoretic studies.

Massorah is a term meaning "tradition," and refers to the tradition by which Jewish scholars (*Massoretes*) tried to pre-

---

1. Karaism is an esoteric Jewish sect, founded in the 700s A.D. by the Hebrew theologian, Anan ben David. It borrows dogmas and principles from Judaism, Christianity, and Islam.

serve faithfully the text of the Old Testament. It embodies a collection of critical notes on the text of the Old Testament, first committed to writing in Tiberias, the capital of Galilee, between the sixth and ninth centuries A.D.. It is a most important work, and it regulated the transmission of Scripture before the invention of the printing press.

Because the Old Testament books were written by hand, no matter how careful the scribes were, mistakes sometimes occurred. When these mistakes were detected by scholarly readers, corrections were made in the form of marginal notes. These annotations were collated and critically considered by Hebrew scholars, who decided upon the correct spelling and pronunciation of Hebrew words. To prevent further mistakes in copying, the scholars counted the chapters, words, and letters of each book, and discussed grammatical rules and accents.

The outcome of Dr. Ginsburg's studies was the publication of the Hebrew text, with his translation of Elias Levita's *Massoreth ha-Massoreth* and Jacob ben Hayim's *Introduction to the Rabbinic Bible*. Four years later he was elected a member of the Board of Revisers of the Old Testament, and he devoted himself to the collation of all the extant remains of the Massorah. With infinite care Dr. Ginsburg collected and digested this vast mass of textual criticism, and presented it in a single volume. As a result it is now possible to consider how far the old manuscripts agree in their variations, additions, and deficiencies. Dr. Ginsburg thus provided an invaluable reference tool for Bible scholars, teachers, and students throughout the world.

So important was this particular work of Dr. Ginsburg considered to be that when his manuscript was sent to Vienna for publication, the British foreign secretary, Lord Salisbury, dispatched it by an official messenger of the queen. The manuscript was far too valuable, and too heavy, for the author himself to convey it by rail, and the risk could not be taken of sending it by any form of carrier service.

In the period 1880–86, Dr. Ginsburg published three volumes of these collations, and with them as a basis edited a new text of the Old Testament for the Trinitarian Bible Society. This was published in 1894 under the title, *The Massoretic-Critical Text of the Hebrew Bible*. In addition, he compiled four various concordances to the Massorah. In 1871 he wrote an elaborate and scholarly account of the Moabite Stone, and was instrumental in exposing certain forgeries.

In 1859, while serving as a missionary in Liverpool, Dr. Ginsburg kept an account of his work, and in his journal records:

> In reviewing my labors of the past year, I find great cause for gratitude and encouragement. Notwithstanding the serious illness I have been visited with, and through which I was laid aside from my work for a considerable time, I have already been privileged to see some cheering results from the twofold work in which I have been engaged. My missionary labors among His brethren, in this new sphere of operation, are gradually extending and increasing proportionately both the sorrows and joy of the laborer, inasmuch as he must, like his Master, sympathize with the temporal as well as with the spiritual wants of the people; and yet, alas! he often is unable to give with the one hand the absolute necessities of the starving body, while endeavoring to administer with the other the bread of life to the perishing soul.

In 1904, on its centennial, the British Bible Society entrusted Ginsburg with the publication of a new critical Hebrew text; it was completed only in 1926. Before his death, however, Ginsburg edited and published the Pentateuch (1908), Isaiah (1909), the Prophets (1911), and Psalms (1913). Ginsburg spent the last years of his life in Middlesex, where he died in 1914.

11

Missionary
to Brazil
1867–1927

Solomon Ginsburg

SOLOMON GINSBURG was born into a deeply religious home, and brought up under a strict religious training. He was born in August, 1867, in Suwalki, Russian Poland, the son of an honored rabbi who hoped that his boy would become a learned Jew and rabbi. But there was very little opportunity for Solomon to obtain a satisfactory education in czarist Russia, so he was sent to his mother's relatives in Koenigsberg, Germany.

After completing his studies at the Liceum he returned home. To his amazement, he learned that his father, without consulting him, had arranged for him to marry the daughter of a wealthy Jew in Suwalki. The dowry and other conditions relating to the marriage were already settled and, apparently, were satisfactory from the families' point of view. Among other benefits arranged was the assurance that Solomon and his wife would live in his father-in-law's house, and that all meals would be provided and all expenses would be met for seven years. This way he could devote his time exclusively to study for the rabbinate without any distracting cares and family responsibilities.

The arrangement seemed attractive. But for Ginsburg there

was a serious complication. The girl was only twelve years of age, and he himself was only fourteen! Such early marriages were not unusual among Jews at this time, but Ginsburg instinctively revolted against the idea. He could not say exactly why this was so, but later he realized that it was God's hand which restrained him from such a union, for God was leading him away from home to distant lands in His service. As preparations were being made for the marriage, Ginsburg fled from home and never saw his father again. Nor did he ever learn what became of the girl.

After leaving home Ginsburg had many adventures and hardships as he made his way from city to city in the hope that one day he would reach the United States. He knew that he had relatives in London, so he decided to go to there first in order to earn enough money for his passage to America. He worked his passage from Hamburg to London in a vessel carrying a cargo of horses, and found the work both difficult and dangerous. He arrived in London, with only three nickels in his pocket, and his uncle received him cordially into his home. He gave Solomon work at a satisfactory wage in his dry goods store.

One Saturday afternoon, while walking in Whitechapel Road, in the Jewish section of London's East End, he was stopped by a Jewish missionary who invited him to hear a sermon for Jews. He accepted the invitation, and heard the gospel for the first time. The preacher took as his text the entire fifty-third chapter of Isaiah. This first glimpse of Christ as the Anointed One and the Savior of mankind marked the turning point in Ginsburg's life.

The message and its impact upon him were strangely and wonderfully related to an incident in his early life, and had not that incident occurred he might not have accepted the missionary's invitation. Told in his own words the incident is of arresting significance:

My father was celebrating the Feast of Tabernacles, sitting in a Succah (Lev. 23:34–43) close to our house. He had a number of visitors, and as I had passed the age of thirteen and was considered a full-fledged Jew, I was allowed to stay and listen to the talks and discussions. Upon the table were several books, among them a well-used copy of the Prophets. Accidentally I opened that book and was reading the fifty-third chapter of Isaiah. There were some comments on the margin and one remark seemed to loom out above all the other scribblings: "To whom does the

Prophet refer in this chapter?" Innocently, I turned to my father and asked him the very same question. He looked at me quite surprised and a profound quietness seemed to come over him. Not being answered I repeated the question, when my father snatched the book out of my hand and slapped me in the face. I felt chagrined and humiliated. I did not like that kind of an answer. But in the providence of God it served its purpose, for when the missionary asked me to go and hear him on that very same chapter, I went out of curiosity to see if he had a better explanation that the one my father had given me.

Because of this incident, so vividly impressed on his memory, Ginsburg was to learn about the Messiah Jesus. As he listened to the missionary unfolding prophecy after prophecy, with Christ as their fulfillment, it seemed that a weight of doubt was lifted from his heart. Faith did not, however, come quickly or easily. For three months he struggled within himself; the struggle was so intense that his health suffered. Finally, on hearing a sermon on Matthew 10:37, "He that loveth father or mother more than Me is not worthy of me," his soul was touched and he resolved to follow Christ at any cost.

When his uncle learned of this decision, he gave Ginsburg a choice: Solomon had to give up his belief in Christ or else lose his position. Solomon refused to give up his belief, and he was driven from his uncle's home. No Jew would hire him, and he wandered through the streets of London for days, friendless and jobless. Observing his predicament, a missionary placed him in a home for Jewish Christians, where he was given instruction in painting.

A year later Solomon received a letter from another uncle who said he had to come to London on business and wished to see him. When they met, his uncle informed him that his "business" in London was to take Solomon home. There was one condition, however. Solomon was to give up his new faith. The uncle warned Solomon that unless he consented to this he was to be excommunicated, disinherited, and considered dead. He was given a week to decide.

Solomon never forgot the horror of that seemingly never-ending week of dark, bitter days and sleepless nights. But the turmoil of his thoughts and the torment of his emotions did not make Solomon waver for one moment in his faith in Christ. In the presence of his uncles and several rabbis he gave his final answer, declaring that he could not compromise with his conscience. On the basis of Hebrew prophecies he had accepted Jesus as the Messiah. He was thereupon cursed and put in Cherem (that is, excommunicated). It was with a heavy heart that he left their presence, full of pity over their mistaken zeal.

Thereafter a great desire rose in Ginsburg's heart to prepare himself for missionary service. After a period of discipline and study, he graduated with honor from Harley College, London. Like the apostle Paul, he felt that his call was to work among Gentiles. This conviction found confirmation in many ways, and he eventually received an invitation to the then-neglected continent of South America. He left for Brazil with no guarantee of support, but he was supremely happy in the realization that he would thus serve his Messiah who had done so much for him.

Brazil was predominantly Roman Catholic, and Solomon was called upon to suffer much persecution from the priest-ridden population. However, his uprightness of character, and his great zeal and love for people won for him a way into their hearts. During his early months in Brazil the foreign mission board of the Southern Baptist Convention in America invited him to join them. They, among others, recognized his versatility, ability, and scholarly attainments, and the force of his witness and missionary endeavors.

In Brazil Dr. Ginsburg was known as "Brother Solomon." Sometimes he was referred to as "the wandering Jew" because of his extensive travels and his itinerant missionary work. Like the "Apostle of the Gentiles" he relied chiefly on his own resources for support—by selling Bibles and tracts to the Catholics!

Dr. Ginsburg quickly gained sufficient fluency in Portuguese (the language of Brazil) to hold open-air services, and taught the people choruses and gospel hymns. At all times he was ready to work with other missionaries who were willing to cooperate with him, for he was not for some time attached to any denomination. In the course of time, however, he met Dr. W. B. Bagby, a veteran Baptist missionary. This was a historic and important encounter, and Solomon was later baptized by Dr. Bagby. On the Sunday following his baptism, Ginsburg was ordained to the Baptist ministry. After this experience and confirmation of his ministry he visited converts whom he had previously baptized by sprinkling and was able to immerse most of them. He spoke of these believers as "those I had led to Christ, but misled on the question of baptism." His most active labors as a Baptist missionary covered the twenty years from 1892 to 1912.

This long and fruitful ministry in Brazil brought many thrilling experiences. There were conflicts with the Catholics; persecutions by and escapes from assassins whom the priests sent to kill him. Many were his afflictions but the Lord delivered him out of them all! He repeatedly told of miraculous escapes from mob attacks, and from being shot at, and he rejoiced in God that he was so wonderfully preserved. His life in Brazil was a "missionary adventure," glorious in its outcome and rich in its evidences of God's grace and care.

Two incidents are especially telling. First, while traveling by train, he sold a Bible to a "nice-looking" young man, and invited him to the open-air meeting in the next town. The meeting lasted from 7:00 p.m. until 3:00 a.m. and was a great success. Tracts were distributed and explained. Questions were asked and answered. Hymns were sung and choruses taught. One such was: "Oh, the blood of Jesus cleanses me." The young man who bought the Bible asked to be taught the entire hymn. But on reaching his home the young man was so afraid of the priest that he gave his Bible away to a baker, to whom also he taught the hymn he had learned. It was a "live coal from the altar of God," resulting in the conversion of the baker and his wife. They buried all their idols, sold their property, and the baker became "a burning torch for God." As a result of the sale of that one Bible there are dozens of churches and preaching places today, proving that "My word shall not return unto Me void . . . ."

The open-air meetings, with singing and distribution of tracts, seemed to reach many people, so Dr. Ginsburg continued them. Often the priests sent rowdy troublemakers to break up the meetings. On such occasions, Dr. Ginsburg said, he prayed hard that God would "keep his tongue quiet and his fists still," for he was a large man himself and could give a good account of himself in a fight. Often he appealed to the police for protection, and seemed always to win out with a Catholic mob.

Ginsburg tells of a time when the priests hired an assassin to "get him" one Sunday afternoon, during an open-air meeting. Even though he knew of the threat to his life, he continued with his plans, trusting God to take care of him. He preached vigorously that day and took plenty of time, waiting for the assassin to appear. Nothing happened, and as night came on he closed the meeting. He later learned that the desperado, in order to find courage for the deed, had drunk some liquor, followed by further draughts, until he fell asleep. "So, king alcohol saved my life" Ginsburg remarked. He then told how the hired assassin came to him, confessed his sins, made a profession of faith, joined the church, and became one of his most faithful helpers and defenders.

Dr. Ginsburg's work with the Baptists was most successful, though often subject to great difficulties and hardships. Every believer was a torch-bearer of the gospel despite the fact that persecutions by the Catholics became increasingly severe. Churches were burned, believers were flogged, and their homes were burned. But such persecutions only gave more power to the gospel and increased its spread. Young converts, full of zeal, scoffed at the Catholic priests.

In a desperate effort the priests stirred up a band of about eight hundred bandits to wipe out the small company of Christians. Twenty-five believers were killed and close to a hundred were wounded. But Dr. Ginsburg obtained an order from the government for protection, the political leader responsible was deposed, and more peaceable times prevailed. The persecution advertised the gospel and the churches entered upon an era of great prosperity, consolidation, and advance. Some congregations reached as many as eight hundred to a thousand.

As the work developed, a class in theology was organized for the teaching and training of converts. Later a day school was established under the charge of Dr. Cannada. This effort so prospered that it was later renamed the "Colegio Americano Baptista," and was very well attended and most successful. Further growth took place when Dr. J. W. Shepard established the Rio College and Seminary, and Dr. Muirhead became director of the Pernambuco College and Seminary. Dr. Ginsburg commented: "Today whole communities rejoice in the God-given freedom of the Gospel."

In the midst of his labors, still dreaming of further conquests for his Messiah, Solomon received the call to higher service. He died on March 31, 1927, after thirty-three years of sacrificial effort in Brazil. He left behind him a notable record of achievement. In a personal tribute, Dr. Entzminger, who was associated with Dr. Ginsburg for many years, wrote:

His going has made Brazil poorer for me, and I think it is no exaggeration to say that no man among us will be so missed by both the missionaries and native Christians as Solomon Ginsburg. He was decidedly the greatest all-round missionary that ever worked in Brazil of any denomination, and will live in the hearts of those whose path he crossed during his noble ministry.

Solomon Ginsburg was a true and valiant ambassador for Christ. Many have continued Ginsburg's labors for the gospel, building upon the foundation he laid. Through his pioneering work and his personal evangelism, many thousands believed in Jesus Christ. Some became workers for Jesus the Messiah, and the powers of darkness and deceit were put to flight. This biography of Dr. Ginsburg, though brief, is sufficient to show that "one with God is a majority." All the priests, politicians, or populace could not prevent or paralyze his witness.

12

Bishop and Educator
1820–1901

Isaac Helmuth

FOR MANY YEARS Poland was the main European reservoir of Jewish orthodoxy, and had one of the largest Jewish communities in Europe. Until shortly before the outbreak of the second world war in 1939, it was also an area of great missionary activity. Warsaw was the chief center of Jewish population, and it was in Warsaw, on December 14, 1820, that Isaac Helmuth was born.

From his earliest years Helmuth's education was most carefully planned, and he received thorough instruction in rabbinical schools, where he reached an advanced degree of learning in biblical and Talmudical subjects. In addition to his traditional Jewish training, Isaac acquired a comprehensive secular knowledge, and in his sixteenth year he was admitted as a student at the University of Breslau. Here he studied classical and Oriental literature.

At the university he was brought into close contact with Dr. S. Neuman, a Hebrew Christian and missionary with the London Society for Promoting Christianity Among the Jews. Through Dr. Neuman, Isaac was led to inquire into the tenets and teachings of the Christian faith. His inquiries led to the early conviction that Christ was the Savior of the world—of Jews and Gentiles alike.

In 1841, when he was only 21 years of age, Helmuth left for England, bearing letters of introduction to the Archbishop of Canterbury. Later he was baptized in All Soul's Church, Liverpool, by the Rev. H. S. Joseph, a missionary of the London Society and a Hebrew Christian. Isaac's conversion and confession of faith were not without severe and heartbreaking cost. His father, on hearing that he had become a Christian, disowned him completely (though after the father's death Isaac's two brothers generously divided the family inheritance with him).

After a three-year course of theological study, Isaac went to Canada. In 1846 Helmuth was ordained to the Christian ministry by Dr. Mountian, bishop of Quebec, and thereafter devoted himself wholeheartedly to his duties as rector of Sherbrook, Quebec. He was also engaged in tutorial work as professor of Hebrew and rabbinical literature at Bishop's College, Lennoxville, and was later appointed to the principalship of the college. In 1853 the Lambeth degree of Doctor of Divinity was conferred upon him. In the same year he was awarded also the honorary degrees of D.C.L., from Trinity College, Toronto, and D.D., from the University of Lennoxville. After eight years as rector and tutor Helmuth resigned both positions upon accepting appointment as general superintendent of the Colonial and Continental Church Society in British North America. When Huron College was opened in 1863, Dr. Helmuth was appointed president, and also became archdeacon of Huron. Huron College faithfully fulfilled its trust under his guidance, and became established as a center of sound teaching. Many devoted ministers of the gospel received the training at the college.

Dr. Helmuth manifested a keen interest in the instruction of youth, and he established a college for boys known as Helmuth Boys' College. He also established a similar institution for young women. Recognition of his ministry and achievements led to his appointment in 1867 as rector of St. Paul's Cathedral and dean of Huron. Four years later he was elected coadjutor to the bishop of Huron, and when the bishop died in 1872, Dr. Helmuth became bishop of the diocese. Despite the increased responsibilities and duties involved in his new appointment, he continued to give special attention to the development and advancement of education, and planned to establish a university in connection with Huron College. In 1880 he visited England to encourage support of the project, and the university was opened on October 5, 1881.

During the twelve years of Dr. Helmuth's episcopate great progress was made in every department of diocesan work. The number of churches rose from 149 to 207, and the number of clergy from 92 to 135; the number of Sunday schools advanced from 110 to 166, and the number of communicants from 4,390 to 8,910.

Dr. Helmuth resigned the see of Huron on March 29, 1883, and returned to England, where he subsequently held various important posts in the church. Failing health compelled his retirement from active work in 1899—at the age of 79.

During the eighteen years he spent in England, Dr. Helmuth was a staunch supporter of Jewish mission work, and often presided over the meetings of the London Jews' Society. It was said of him:

> His solid learning, acquaintance with the languages and modes of thought of his own people, sound common sense, and prudent consel, as well as his urbanity and courtesy, made him an ideal chairman. His sterling qualities of heart and mind, his confiding nature, buoyant temperament, and his bright and happy face always infused sunshine wherever he went.

While his labors as bishop in Canada were successful, his usefulness in England was even greater and more satisfactory to himself. He published several outstanding works, including *The Genuineness and Authenticity of the Pentateuch*, and *The Divine Dispensation*, a critical commentary on the Hebrew Scriptures. His *Biblical Thesaurus* was a literal translation and critical analysis of every word in the original language of the Old Testament, with explanatory notes and appendices. Among his minor contributions to literature were: *The Everlasting Nation* and *The Spirit of Prophecy*.

Even though his accomplishments were great, Helmuth's personality remained sweet:

> To know him was indeed to love him, as well as to honor and to esteem him. His sweet and gentle nature, his amiable disposition, his beautiful character, his fatherly attitude, and his unfailing tenderness and sympathy, have indelibly associated him in our mind with the beloved disciple St. John, whose last words would have been natural indeed upon his lips: "Little children, love one another."

There was a true and transparent saintliness about Dr. Helmuth in his attitude toward all men, but especially those of the household of faith.

Holy Scripture counsels, "Mark the perfect man, . . . for the end of that man is peace" (Ps. 37:37). Dr. Helmuth passed peacefully into the presence of the Lord on May 28, 1901 at the age of eighty.

13

William Herschel

SEVERAL HEBREW CHRISTIANS bore the honored name of Herschel, though they were not all of the same family group. None was more distinguished than Sir William Herschel, who was appointed Astronomer Royal by King George III. William was born on November 15, 1738, in Hanover which was at that time under the British Crown. He died in England on August 22, 1822.

Little is known of his early life, except that his father desired him to become a musician and arranged his education accordingly. At the age of seventeen, Herschel was a soldier in the Hanoverian Guards, and in 1755 he traveled to England with the Guards' band. It is not known exactly when he became a Christian or when he was baptized, but five years after his arrival in England he was a church organist at Bath in Somerset.

During his period of service with the Hanoverian Guards, Herschel yearned for a quiet way of life, away from wars and rough companions. He longed to devote his time and talents to the gentler aspects of life. He therefore deserted his company, and soon afterward began his researches in astronomy, earning his living by teaching music. But he lived in a state of constant anxiety. He was troubled by feelings of guilt for deserting the King's Guards. He was continually afraid of discovery and punishment for desertion, the penalty of which at that time was death.

After he had reached a position of great fame and influence in science, Herschel was summoned to Windsor Castle to present himself to King George III. The king wished to hear from him details of his discoveries. At the appointed time he presented himself at court. As he advanced toward the king and the distinguished company there assembled, his heart raced in apprehension. He was a delinquent, a deserter who had not been pardoned or acquitted. He feared that he might be exposed and thrown into prison. But the king rose from the throne to greet him. When they met, the king spoke kindly to him, "Before we can discuss science, there is a little matter of business that must be disposed of." As he spoke he handed to Sir William a document signed and sealed with the royal warrant.

Sir William had no idea what the sealed document contained, but he was sure the king could not possibly know of his desertion. His amazement was therefore all the greater when, on reading the document, he discovered that it was the king's pardon, written in his own hand! He was now a free man, no longer under the condemnation of the law, no longer guilty and liable to die for his wrongdoing. He could not have had a greater or clearer illustration in his own experience of the grace of God in His mercy toward the guilty.

For some time Herschel had earned his living by teaching, and had devoted most of his spare time to the study of astronomy and the construction of telescopes. It was with one of these telescopes that he discovered the planet Uranus in March, 1781. This was a discovery of great importance in the science of astronomy at that time, since only five of the planets were then known and identified. His fame spread, and he was acknowledged as one of the greatest scientists of the age. He was made an honorary member of most European scientific societies, and his abilities and contributions were recognized by his appointment as Astronomer Royal. He was knighted in 1816.

In reviewing the life and accomplishments of Sir William Herschel, some reference should be made to his devoted sister Caroline Lucretia, without whose help and understanding he might not have achieved as much in his research. It was she who wrote down his notes, read to him from many works of reference, and sometimes, when his hands were busy manipulating the telescope, she even fed him. In time, she also gained a reputation as a capable astronomer. In 1828 she received the medal of the Astronomical Society for her catalogue of nebulae. She also discovered eight comets. (Sir William also had a son who was knighted, Sir John Frederick William Herschel, an outstanding scientist.)

Sir William is considered the father of sidereal science. Three times he made a complete review of the northern heavens, and fixed the positions of 2500 nebulae, of which only 103 had been previously known. He was the first to deduce by inference the existence of double stars, that is, pairs of stars that revolve around a common center. He identified and described 209 such binary stars. He was the first to define and explain the composition of the Milky Way, and its relation to the universe in general. His views on the position of our solar system in relation to the Milky Way are the basis for the modern theory of the constitution of the universe. Herschel is also known as the discoverer of the infrared rays of the sun. These and other discoveries, along with his explanations of many of the mysteries of the heavens, earned him a prominent place among the great men of science.

14

Missionary
1807–1864

Haymin Herschell

WORLD EVANGELIZATION owes much to the courageous and uncompromising witness and missionary enterprise of Hayim Herschell, especially in the field of Jewish missions. His birthplace was Strzelno, in what was then Prussian Poland, and the date of his birth April 7, 1807. He was the fourth child in a family of twelve children of which ten were boys and two were girls. His education, and that of his brothers, was the kind of training provided by all pious, God-fearing Jewish parents of that time.

Very early in life Herschell manifested a desire to give his life to the service of God and His people. In the hope of becoming a rabbi, he devoted his early youth to rabbinical studies, but God had chosen him for another and greater task. Like Paul the apostle he could claim that he was separated and set apart from the day of his birth. His own words testify to his deep spiritual sensitivity and awareness:

> I was taught to repeat the morning and evening prayers with great solemnity, and on the feast days my attention was particularly drawn to the impressive confession in our liturgy, "It is

99

because of our sins we are driven away from our land." On the Day of Atonement I used to see my devout parents weep when they repeated the pathetic confession that follows the enumeration of the sacrifices which were appointed by God to be offered for the sins of omission. Many a time I shed sympathetic tears as I joined them in saying that we had now no temple, no high priest, no altar, and no sacrifices. As I advanced in years and understanding, my religious impressions became stronger; fear and trembling often took hold of me; and what was my refuge, what the balm for my wounded spirit?

His sense of his own sinfulness as well as the sinfulness of his people gave him no rest. He sought to calm his distress with prayer and the study of the Talmud and other sacred books, but all to no avail.

In his restlessness he left home at the age of fifteen, and went to study at the Berlin University. But he found no peace there. On the contrary, his Jewish faith was seriously shaken by the encroachments of modern thought. Finding Berlin a threat to his peace of mind and religious views, he left the city for Hamburg. During the journey from the German capital to the northern seaport, he befriended a man who gave him letters of introduction to friends in London. His disturbed and restless spirit drove him from place to place, and in his search for truth and peace he traveled to London, Berlin, and Paris.

While in Paris he learned of the death of his mother, and was plunged into deeper despair, as he touchingly records:

> One day I was in acute distress of mind, feeling, as David expresses it, that I had sunk in deep mire where there is no standing. All my own efforts to free myself were of no avail. My struggles only made me sink deeper and deeper. For the first time in my life I prayed extemporaneously. [The Jewish custom is to recite standard written prayers, not to call upon God in spontaneously chosen words.] I cried out, "O God, I have no one to help me, and I dare not approach Thee, for I am guilty. Help, O help me; for the sake of my father Abraham who was willing to offer up his son Isaac, have mercy upon me and impute his righteousness unto me." But there was no answer from God; no peace to my wounded spirit. I felt as if God had forsaken me, as if the Lord had cast me off forever and would be favorable no more.

But God does not forsake those who pray for His help. A few days after his urgent and despairing cry his attention was drawn to a New Testament passage which he saw on the printed wrapper of an article he had bought. He did not know then that the words were, in fact, the Beatitudes given in the Sermon on the Mount, and he wished he could find the book in which these comforting words were found.

In the overruling providence and loving purpose of God, he was later guided to the house of a friend, where he saw a copy of the New Testament. He writes:

> Impelled by curiosity I took it up, and in turning over the leaves beheld the very passage that had interested me so much. I immediately borrowed it and began to read it with great avidity. At first I felt quite bewildered and was so shocked by the constant recurrence of the name of Jesus that I cast the book aside. At length I determined to read it through. . . . In reading the account of the crucifixion, the meekness and love of Jesus of Nazareth astonished me, and the cruel hatred manifested against Him by the priests and rulers in Israel excited within me a feeling of compassion for Him and of indignation against His murderers. But I did not as yet see any connection between the sufferings of Jesus and my sins.

At last, however, the connection became clear to him, and he was unshakably convinced that Jesus was the Messiah, and that the New Testament, equally with the Old Testament, was the Word of God. The time came when he was able to cry out, "Lord, I believe Jesus is the Messiah, the Redeemer and King of Israel, who was wounded for our transgressions and bruised for our iniquities. For His sake have mercy upon me and give me peace." His prayer was heard and he found his peace through and in "the Prince of peace."

At the age of 21 he entered the Operative Jewish Converts' Institution in London. On April 14, 1830, he was baptized, taking as his baptismal name the name of his godfather, the Rev. Henry C. Ridley; he was thereafter known as Ridley H. Herschell. Afterward he was ordained to the Baptist ministry and worked zealously for the conversion of his Jewish brethren to the true faith. He did, in fact, lead five of his brothers to Christ, and took a strong initiative in arousing Christian interest in the cause of Jewish evangelization.

On November 7, 1842, Herschell convened a meeting in London for the purpose of founding the British Society for the Propagation of the Gospel Among the Jews, and which was attended by the Rev. Robert Murray McCheyne. Later, a worker of the new society founded the Mildmay Mission to the Jews, and through workers in that mission sprang the Hebrew Chris-

tian Testimony to Israel and the Society for Distributing the
Holy Scripture to the Jews. Herschell was closely associated
with this work until his death in 1864.

In additon to his missionary interest, Herschell was also concerned for the welfare of Hebrew Christians. He founded a
home to which Jews were admitted who were known to be
seeking the truth as it is in Jesus. With the cooperation of Sir
Culling Eardley-Eardley, Herschell built Trinity Chapel, Regent
Street, London, where he was truly a father in God to Jewish
converts. His love for his brethren in Christ was warmly recip-
rocated, and sixty Hebrew Christians presented him with a
Polyglot Bible. The society Dr. Herschell founded operated initially in England and in eastern Europe, but ultimately it so
developed its witness throughout the world that it was renamed the International Society for the Evangelization of the
Jews.

Dr. Herschell's attachment to and regard for his fellow Jews
never diminished. He did all in his power to ensure their welfare, and established a benevolent fund for the alleviation of the
suffering of destitute foreign Jews. Dr. Herschell also engaged
in some literary activity. Among his publications are: *A Brief
Sketch of the State and Expectations of the Jews* (1837); *Plain
Reasons Why I, a Jew Have Become a Catholic and Not a Roman
Catholic* (1842); *A Visit to My Fatherland: Notes of a Journey to
Syria and Palestine* (1844). In addition, he edited a periodical
called *Voice of Israel,* and wrote several books designed to
further the propagation of the gospel.

In order to advance the spread of the gospel among the Jews,
Herschell undertook several long journeys and had the joy of
seeing many Jews become believers and servants of God. Of his
five brothers whom he led to Christ, three became ministers of
the gospel. And there were other relatives and friends who
were converted, and who became either ministers or missionaries to the Jews.

The Herschell family produced many outstanding men
whose names are recorded in the annals of human progress.
Among them was his son, Lord Farrer Herschell.[1]

1. Lord Farrer Herschell was born in 1837. At the age of 20, after studying
in Germany at the University of Bonn, Farrer took his degree at London
University. In 1860 he was called to the Bar, and later held various important
public positions. In 1874 he was elected Member of Parliament for the City
of Durham. In 1880 he became Solicitor General during Gladstone's premier-

Dr. Hayim Herschell's dedication and devotion to his work was greatly honored and respected during his lifetime, and many fine tributes were paid after his death. Grateful Hebrew Christians all over the world, and his many Gentile friends, accorded him appreciation and recognition for his labors. He passed away on May 14, 1864, at the age of 57. Among the many mourners in the long procession that accompanied his body to its final resting place were five hundred policemen for whom he had held a weekly Bible class. Shortly before he died he remarked: "It is wonderful to look back and see how literally true it is that goodness and mercy have followed me all the days of my life. Every step has been mercy. I should have made shipwreck over and over again if He had not saved me."

---

ship, and was knighted. Six years later he was made a baron, and became Lord Chancellor.

Lord Herschell was highly esteemed in public affairs, and held many high positions, including the presidency of the Imperial Institute. His speeches were characterised by a combination of lucidity, acuteness, and persuasiveness. His remarkable intellectual gifts were devoted not only to public matters, but also to the glory of God, for he was an earnest and active Christian and a staunch churchman. He was a warden of St. Peter's Church, Eaton Square.

Toward the end of his life he was entrusted with the important commission to settle questions pending between England and the United States, one of which was the settlement of the boundary between Alaska and Canada. He died in Washington in 1899, while working on this commission.

15

Preacher and Educator 1813–1874

Ludwig Jacoby

LUDWIG JACOBY was a German Jew, the son of devout and devoted parents. He was born in the German town of Mecklenburg in 1813. When he grew older his parents apprenticed him to a Hamburg merchant, for whom he became a traveling salesman. In this itinerant work he came into contact with many Christians, and was intrigued by their qualities of character and lifestyle compared to the familiar Jewish ways. Observing that Christians were quite different from what he and other Jewish children were taught about them, Jacoby began to inquire about the Christian faith. His inquiries convinced him that Jesus of Nazareth was indeed the Messiah of Israel, and the Redeemer of all mankind. Conviction soon became saving faith.

As his work developed he traveled to England and, ultimately, to America. While working in Cincinnati he chanced to hear the renowned Methodist preacher William Nast. On Christmas Eve, 1839, Jacoby joined the Methodist church and was "licensed to exhort." Ten days after his conversion he had written in glowing terms about prayer meetings to friends in Germany: "My only wish is that all my fellow German countrymen could see the joy that prevails in such meetings, and if their hearts were not made of stone they certainly could not resist the Spirit of God."

Jacoby married Amelia Theresa Nuelsen, also a Methodist. Together in the service of the Lord they experienced both the tests and the triumphs of faith. In 1841, with their five-week-old daughter, they traveled by riverboat to St. Louis, Missouri. Jacoby sought a location in the city to begin his ministry. He found an abandoned Presbyterian church building and occupied it in order to hold services. Jacoby and his wife waited, but no one came to his meetings. So one Sunday, Jacoby began ringing the church bells vigorously. Within a short time, people came to the church to see what was happening. This was how Jacoby assembled his first congregation for the first Methodist church west of the Mississippi.

In the early days at St. Louis, Jacoby encountered many difficulties and met with many obstructions. Ruffians fired pistols in the congregation, smeared the church steps with tar, and tossed rocks through the windows. But Jacoby persevered. Within three months the church had twenty-two members, and within a year his congregation built its own church at a cost of twelve hundred dollars—a large sum in those days. For his labors Jacoby received an annual salary of two hundred dollars. So great was the progress of the work that two more congregations were established in other parts of the city.

But Jacoby did not confine himself exclusively to his spiritual ministry. He was greatly interested in matters of education, particularly for the large numbers of German settlers in St. Louis. He helped in the foundation of German day schools where English was taught. This was the only education available to immigrant families who did not understand English. Jacoby also wrote an English-German grammar which became a standard textbook for immigrants.

After working in St. Louis for some years, Jacoby returned to Germany as a propagandist for Methodism according to John Wesley, "salvation by the grace of God." As a result of his efforts, churches, orphanages, and missions were established in both Germany and Switzerland. Eventually, Jacoby felt that his work in Europe was completed, and that he was needed in the western United States. He therefore returned to America to preach and to work. Salem Church, the first church Jacoby built and built up in St. Louis, continued to prosper and, in 1873, a new church building was erected. Numerous missionaries and ministers went forth from this church, including Jacoby's nephew John L. Nuelsen, who became a bishop.

Jacoby died in October, 1874, at the age of sixty-one, and was buried in the Old Salem Cemetery. Later, when town development engulfed the old cemetery, his grave and that of his wife were removed to Valhalla Cemetery. Eighty-two years later, on Sunday, May 13, 1956, a memorial shrine was erected over their graves. This impressive ceremony took place in the presence of members of the Salem Methodist Church which Jacoby founded, and also in the presence of many people from other churches. They all desired to pay tribute to a son of Israel who had dedicated his life to the spread of the gospel.

16

Theologian, Writer,
and Teacher
1803–1886

Christian
Andreas Herman
Kalkar

"YE HAVE NOT chosen me, but I have chosen you, and ordained you, that ye should go and bring forth fruit" (John 15:16). These words of Christ are especially apt when applied to Dr. Christian Andreas Herman Kalkar. He was a Swedish Jew, born in Stockholm on November 27, 1803. His father, a rabbi, was personally responsible for his early education, and one of his brothers was a well-known and respected Talmudist and Hebrew poet. When Kalkar was only nine years of age his father died, and he went to live with his uncle, who was a lawyer in Copenhagen. His uncle provided an excellent education, and so great were Kalkar's abilities that at the age of seventeen he was able to enter the university to study law.

The contrast between his former rabbinic education and the influence of his new surroundings greatly troubled him. His association with Christians led him to think highly of the claims of Christianity that in his early life he had been taught and had learned to abhor. His considerations and inquiries led him to the conviction that Jesus of Nazareth was his Savior, and so he turned to Him for refuge. Kalkar was baptized in 1823, when he was twenty years of age.

Following his conversion, the study of law lost its attraction for him, and he devoted his time to the study of theology and philosophy. After the completion of his course at the university, Kalkar spent sixteen years teaching in various high schools. During that period he published several works on various books of the Old Testament, on the Reformation in Denmark, and his highly-prized *Manual of Devotion*.

In 1836 Kalkar received the degree of Doctor of Theology, and was later appointed to a country parish near Copenhagen. After twenty-five years, when his health was no longer equal to the demands of his charge, he resigned, and in his retirement again devoted himself to literary work. Among the important fruits of his literary labors was a translation of the Bible into Danish (accomplished with the assistance of two other divines) and *Life Pictures from the History of the Kingdom of God*.

But the most important work of Kalkar's later years was the service he rendered to the missionary cause. In 1871 he was elected president of the Danish Missionary Society. Under his skillful and dedicated leadership this society made great progress at home and abroad. Kalkar awakened throughout the country a keen interest in mission work through the conferences which he initiated. His *History of Missions to the Heathen* received wide recognition and acceptance, and was translated into German. In addition to this general treatment of missions he wrote a history of Jewish missionary work, which was translated into German under the title *Israel and the Church*.

Kalkar did much to bring about a more balanced and exact appreciation of the state of church affairs in Denmark. Through his *Theological Journal* he succeeded in healing the divisions among Protestants in his own country, and did much to lessen the bitterness of their controversies and conflicts. In his own home, representatives of diverse parties met in tolerant and friendly association.

Dr. Kalkar enjoyed the confidence and friendship of the queen of Denmark, who corresponded with him regularly. His home life, with his wife Dorothea Tryde and his children, was exceptionally happy. He retained a wonderful freshness of spirit even in old age. This was evident to all who observed him at the Evangelical Alliance Meeting in Copenhagen in 1884. Dr. Kalkar was then eighty-one years of age, and presided with dignity and charm over this extraordinary assembly of Christians from all parts of the world. One observer commented that this Hebrew Christian was "a fine prophetic picture of the future, when Israel, converted to Christ, shall take her stand in front of all other nations, calling upon all to join in the praise of their common Savior."

In his eighty-third year, Dr. Kalkar became seriously ill and it was evident that the end was drawing near. His last night on earth was spent in prayer and in reciting texts of Scripture. On the following morning he passed peacefully into the presence of the Lord. His death was mourned by multitudes, by high and low alike. His memory remains as a witness that God has not forsaken Israel, and that His covenant with this everlasting nation is operative, valid and unchangeable: "He abideth faithful."

17

German Baptist
1806–1884

Julius Kobner

SOLOMON KOBNER was the son of Isaac Aaron Kobner, a Jew from Lissa, Poland. Isaac moved to Odense, Denmark, where Solomon was born in 1806. Isaac Kobner was the religious leader of the Jewish community in Odense, and Solomon was educated with a view to his becoming a rabbi. But his heart was not in the Judaism he was taught. Its laws and customs held no appeal for him, and the prayers he had to memorize seemed unnatural and formal.

Early in life Solomon left Denmark for Germany, where he learned the printing and engraving trades. In these he excelled, and even devised technical and mechanical improvements, for which he received an award. But, despite the demands of his work, he did not neglect his general education, and continued to study. He was especially gifted in the study and learning of languages. He had a great love for poetry and was himself an accomplished poet. (When he became a Christian this aptitude was devoted to the writing of Christian hymns.)

Kobner's favorite study, even from childhood, was the Bible. Through it he was led step by step to the conviction that Jesus of Nazareth was indeed "Him of whom Moses in the Law, and the prophets did write." Nevertheless, he found it extremely difficult to take the step of baptism. During a visit to Lubeck he got in touch with the pastor of the Reformed Church, seeking guidance in the Christian faith.

This contact proved to be one of the most significant in his life, and shortly afterward he moved to Hamburg. In the summer of 1826, at the age of twenty, Kobner was baptized in a Lutheran church, and adopted the name Julius Johann Wilhelm. While in Hamburg he worked as an engraver, and also spent much of his time teaching languages. Among his pupils was Juliana von Schroter, the nineteen-year-old daughter of a German officer. Julius and Juliana decided to marry, and sought the consent of their parents. When this was refused, Julius appealed to the king of Denmark, from whom he secured a special license for the wedding.

It was chiefly through his wife that Julius Kobner became a convinced and active Baptist. While on a shopping expedition, Juliana heard of the evangelistic work of Johann Gerhard Oncken, a colporteur and evangelist of the Edinburgh Bible Society. Oncken's activities had aroused considerable discussion among the populace and, after much persuasion, Juliana prevailed upon her husband to go with her to hear the evangelist preach. As a result of what he heard, Julius' religious life underwent a complete and vital transformation. This led to his rebaptism by immersion, and he joined the Baptist church.

Oncken quickly became aware of Kobner's abilities and sought his help, which was readily and enthusiastically given. Kobner's Jewish training provided him with an extensive knowledge of the Hebrew Scriptures, and he was soon recognized as one of the three great pioneers and leaders of the German Baptist movement, along with Johann Gerhard Oncken and Gottfried Wilhelm Lehman. Their labors in extending and and establishing the German Baptist cause met with extraordinary success.

But their efforts were not without frustrations and hindrances. The movement encountered bitter opposition, and its adherents met with severe persecution by both the civil and religious authorities, and sometimes at the hands of incited mobs. Kobner and Oncken were imprisoned, but even from prison Kobner continued his work. To one of his fellow laborers he sent a message concealed in a loaf of bread, giving a list of the places where believers were meeting in secret. He also used the time of his imprisonment to complete valuable literary work.

In spite of the sustained and fierce opposition, the Baptist movement throughout Germany grew rapidly. In 1849 it held its first *Bundes Konferenz*, when thirty-six churches were represented. Twenty-one years later the number of churches had risen to ninety-two.

The work was most carefully planned and energetically carried out. Oncken organized and directed the missionary effort, while Kobner busied himself as an itinerant preacher. He was an effective speaker and was greatly sought after for pulpit and platform. He also wrote many notable and inspiring hymns, which were collected and published for congregational singing in 1840.

Oncken's maxim was, "Every Baptist a missionary." In pursuit of this ideal and the spread of the gospel throughout Europe, it was decided that Oncken should stay in Germany, and that Kobner should return to Denmark to establish a witness there.

In Copenhagen, Kobner found himself handicapped by the law which prohibited secession from the state church. He went back to Hamburg, but later he and Oncken returned to Denmark to engage in a joint effort. On October 30, 1839, they baptized eleven people, and thereby formed the first Baptist church in Copenhagen. The members of the new church were, however, exposed to ridicule and severe persecution. For a time, member families with infants were heavily fined for every day their children remained unbaptized in the state church. Many were brought to economic ruin by these heavy fines.

Despite the persecution and victimization, the Baptist movement in Denmark grew in numerical and spiritual strength. Many people were baptized, and new churches were formed in several parts of the country. Fellow Baptists in other countries came to help their Danish brethren.

In 1841 British Baptists sent a delegation to Copenhagen to plead for tolerance for the local Baptists. The delegation was highly commended by the clergy of all English denominations as well as by high-ranking officials in the British government. The delegates were received by both the king of Denmark, King Christian VIII, and the head of the state church, Bishop Mynster. The king was sympathetic and attentive, but the bishop remained stern and unrelenting. The appeal of the delegation was not entirely futile, however. Baptists were allowed to exist and worship in a few out-of-the-way areas where it was felt they were unlikely to exercise much influence. The following year a delegation of American Baptists made a strong appeal for tolerance and freedom of worship, but was no more successful than the British delegation.

Kobner was formally ordained to the German Baptist ministry in 1844, and was given the title "Missionary to Germany." He traveled extensively throughout Germany and neighboring countries. In 1847, he wrote a vigorous pamphlet called, *Manifesto to the German People,* calling upon them to allow religious toleration and freedom for every man and woman on German soil, whether they were Christians, Jews, Moslems, or any other religion. This desire for individual liberty was a ruling and motivating factor in Kobner's life.

As the work grew, Kobner advanced to the forefront of the Baptist movement in Germany and other parts of Europe. With Gottfried Lehman, he sought to link together all evangelical Christians. They attended the Evangelical Alliance Conference in Paris in 1855, during the Great Exhibition. After that, Kobner visited England to appeal for financial help for the training of young men for the ministry. He also assisted Oncken by conducting courses of study at Barmen in German history, world history, church history, physics, geology, and astronomy.

Returning to Denmark where the work continued to prosper, Kobner edited a hymnbook for the movement there, writing most of the hymns himself. When there was dissension within or among the churches Kobner was often called upon to mediate or to guide the differing factions to an acceptable solution. And there were occasions when he had to take the opposite view from his friend Oncken.

From the years 1865 to 1879 Kobner was pastor of a Baptist church in Copenhagen. In 1867 he organized the building of a church in Copenhagen with a seating capacity of six hundred—it remains the largest Baptist church in Denmark to this day.

Kobner was unceasingly active in the service of Christ and His people, and undertook many long and wearisome journeys in His cause. In those days, such journeys were quite hazardous. Traveling in open carts, exposed to wind and rain, with poor sleeping quarters and dimly-lighted rooms—not to mention the discomfort of bad roads—demanded stamina, determination, and zeal. These Kobner manifested to an extreme degree. And, in additon to meeting the needs of the churches, Kobner produced much valuable literary work.

Appreciative reference was made to his literary work in a 1929 issue of the *Baptist Quarterly:*

> The German Baptist Hymn Book contains fifty of Kobner's hymns. Some few are worthy of comparison with the work of Zinzendorf and Tersteegen; all of them are of vigorous and obvious sincerity and piety.
>
> [Kobner also wrote] *The Waldensians*, a poetical drama, published in 1861. Kobner was evidently drawn to a study of the Waldensians by the belief that their kinship with the early church and with the later Baptists was close. He aimed at giving a true historical picture.... Kobner's work ... is dominated by the conception that world history is God's drama.
>
> *Manifesto to the German People* (1848) ... deals with the relations of church and state. [It] was written at a time when public opinion was excited over the question of religious freedom.... Kobner rejects any idea of state connection or establishment; it leads, he urges, both within and without the Church, to the method of the Inquisition.
>
> *A pamphlet on Sanctification*, issued in 1855, [was] inspired by the seventh chapter of Romans. It is clear from this that Kobner had had a much wider conception of Christian fellowship and Christian duty than might be suggested by his resolute independency.[1]

In addition to the literary productions referred to above, Kobner wrote seven small volumes on theological subjects, setting forth his views on miracles, eschatology, the New Testament church, the sin against the Holy Ghost, church government, and the relations of church and state. He also wrote a prose poem for his small daughter, entitled *The Violin Player*.

In 1882 Kobner's friend and colleague Gottfried Lehman passed away, and he was invited to succeed him as pastor of the Berlin church. Without hesitation he accepted the invitation, although he was then seventy-six years old. Two years after Lehman's death news reached Kobner that Oncken had died in Switzerland, leaving him the sole survivor of the "cloverleaf" trio of German Baptist pioneers. At Oncken's funeral in Hamburg, Kobner preached the graveside oration. Unfortunately, at

---

1. "Julius Kobner and the German Baptists," in *Baptist Quarterly*, vol. 4, no. 8, October, 1929.

the graveside he caught a chill which confined him to his bed. From this illness he never recovered, and in February, 1884, he passed away.

On the hundredth anniversary of Kobner's birth, one hundred of his choicest sermons were published in the press under the title *Lebens Wasser* (Living Water). In Copenhagen there is a beautiful church known as the Julius Kobner Kirche, in honor of his memory.

The influence of Kobner's life is still felt in Europe, in both its quality and its labors. It was said at his funeral that he was "an Israelite indeed in whom is no guile."

18

Author,
Hebrew-Christian
Leader
1882–1936

Leon Levison

ACCORDING TO Jewish tradition there are four "sacred cities" in Israel: Jerusalem, Hebron, Tiberias, and Safed. Safed lies about seven and a half miles northwest of Lake Tiberias, and stands approximately 2800 feet above sea level. In the time of Christ it was the site of a rabbinical school of some importance, and it was here, in 1882, that Leon Levison was born. Leon was the fourth son of Rabbi Nahum Levison, who was renowned among his people as a profound expositor of the principles of Jewish law and custom. Growing up as he did in such a religious home, Leon naturally and eagerly imbibed the rich knowledge and culture of his father, and of his Jewish environment.

He was also greatly influenced by the rich learning and piety of his saintly teacher, Rabbi Joshua. But he was not satisfied with only intellectual pursuits. He desired to engage in and achieve through manual work. To this end he became an agricultural worker, and did some successful experiments with grapes.

Being a natural leader, Levison distinguished himself from the young men of the town. He succeeded in uniting them in a single group which rendered very useful service to the community. In order, as he said, "to know what other people think," he learned French, the cultural and commercial language of the Near East at that time. These studies brought him into contact with missionaries of the Free Church of Scotland who had a school in Safed. From them he learned English and, most important of all, the story of Jesus the Nazarene. Leon undertook these studies secretly, at night, for fear of his people, who hated and despised the missionaries, and relentlessly persecuted any Jew who associated with them.

Leon was only nineteen years old when he came under the influence of these Christians, and at the suggestion of Dr. George Wilson, the church's medical missionary in Palestine, went to Scotland. Within a few months he was publicly baptized in the Barclay church, and thus began his service for Christ and the Jews. For two years he worked in a factory to earn his living, and in his spare time he worked for the medical mission among the Jews of Edinburgh. In order to fit himself for more effective Christian work he studied at the University of Edinburgh and at New College.

Following this preparation, Levison worked for thirty years as the church's representative. One of the most important and effective aspects of his work was the discussions carried out in his own home, where many Jews were won for Christ. Levison was an able speaker and effective preacher, and traveled throughout the length and breadth of Scotland arousing the church in the cause of Jewish missions.

During the first world war Levison engaged in political and economic activities for which he was knighted in 1919. He also distinguished himself in his endeavors for the Russian Jewish Relief Fund, and in connection with a fund to aid Palestinian Jews. To help his needy brethren he succeeded in raising £200,000, an extremely large sum in those days. In addition to these activities he rendered valuable secret service for the British government in Palestine. Both his official and his public service gained recognition, for in addition to the knighthood conferred upon him he was presented with the Freedom of the City of Edinburgh in 1923; he became a Knight of the Star and the Cross of the Church of the Holy Sepulchre; and he received the Imperial Order of Russia. Notwithstanding these honors, however, he remained a humble, devout servant of the Master.

Throughout his life, Sir Leon devoted his time and energy to a variety of interests and activities. He was chairman and director of the publishing house of Marshall, Morgan and Scott. He wrote several books, including *The Life of Paul*. His special interest, however, was in Jewish evangelization, and the binding together of Hebrew Christians in a common fellowship. To this end he founded the International Hebrew Christian Alliance, which now has branches in all parts of the world. Through this fellowship Hebrew Christians find help in the difficulties and dangers which so often befall Jews who accept Christ as their Messiah.

Sir Leon had a great vision of the kingdom of God, and of what the converted Jew could do for the cause of Christ. In his lifetime Levison was universally honored, and was held in great respect by people of all classes, though some Jewish leaders resented his success in winning Jews for Christ. None of their criticism moved him, however, and the sufferings and sorrows of Israel continued to weigh heavily upon him.

This burden of concern, together with his intense labors for his brethren according to the flesh, aged Sir Leon prematurely, and he died suddenly on November 25, 1936, at the age of 54. The many tributes expressed in his memory included one from a leading member of the International Hebrew Christian Alliance:

> No Hebrew Christian in modern times was so universally respected, so highly honored, and so deeply loved as our esteemed president. Equally true is it that no Hebrew Christian since the days of the apostle Paul loved and served his Lord and his people more wholeheartedly, and in more self-forgetful devotion than did Sir Leon.
>
> In the passing of Sir Leon Levison the church has lost a Christian statesman, our Hebrew Christian movement an illustrious leader, and Hebrew Christians throughout the world will keenly miss him as they would a father, a brother, and a friend.

19

Rabbi and Writer
1824–1909

Iechiel Lichtenstein

AFTER FORTY YEARS as district rabbi in Tapio Szele, Hungary, Rabbi Iechiel Lichtenstein read the New Testament. Through his reading and the working of the Holy Spirit in mind and heart, he found Him of whom all the Scriptures testify. His response was immediate and complete, and he accepted Jesus Christ as his Savior and as the Messiah of Israel.

As Rabbi Lichtenstein progressed in the knowledge of Christ he boldly communicated his new-found truth to his congregation in the synagogue, and in his sermons made frequent references to the New Testament. His efforts however, were not wholly acceptable to his congregation, and some members accused him to the chief rabbi in Budapest concerning his Christian belief and preaching. This brought about his resignation as rabbi and resulted in severe hardship and persecution. But he continued to preach the gospel, and maintained a courageous and consistent witness.

As his knowledge of Christ increased and his Christian experience developed, he became a prolific writer. In a pamphlet entitled *A Jewish Mirror* he tells of his first reading of the New Testament and of its effect upon him:

Impressions of early life take a deep hold, and as in my riper years I still had no cause to modify these impressions, it is no wonder that I came to think that Christ Himself was the plague and curse of the Jews, the origin and promoter of our sorrows and persecutions. In this conviction I grew to years of manhood, and still cherishing it I became old. I knew no difference between true and merely nominal Christianity. Of the fountainhead of Christianity I knew nothing. Strangely enough, it was the horrible Tisza-Eszlar blood accusation[1] which first drew me to read the New Testament. This trial brought from their lurking places all the enemies of the Jews, and once again as in olden times, the cry reechoed: "Death to the Jew!" The frenzy was excessive, and among the ring-leaders were many who used the name of Christ and His doctrine as a cloak to cover their abominable doings.

These wicked practices of men, wearing the name of Christ only to further their evil designs, aroused the indignation of the true Christians who, with pen on fire, and warning voices, denounced the lying rage of the anti-Semites. In articles written by the latter in defense of the Jews, I often met with passages where Christ was spoken of as He who brings joy to men, the Prince of Peace and the Redeemer; and his gospel was extolled as a message of love and life to all people.

I was surprised, and scarcely trusting my eyes, I took a New Testament out of its hidden corner; a book which some forty years before I had in vexation taken from a Jewish teacher, and I began to turn over its leaves to read. How can I express the impression which I then received? The half had not been told me of the greatness, power, and glory of this book, formerly a sealed book to me. All seemed so new to me and yet it did me good like the sight of an old friend, who has laid aside his dusty, travel-worn graments, and appears in festal attire.

In his pamphlet *Judaism and Christianity* he writes:

I had thought the New Testament to be impure, a source of pride, of selfishness, of hatred, and of the worst kind of violence, but as I opened it I felt myself peculiarly and wonderfully taken possession of. A sudden glory, a light flashed through my soul. I looked for thorns and found roses; I discovered pearls instead of pebbles; instead of hatred love; instead of vengeance forgiveness; instead of bondage freedom; instead of pride humility; conciliation instead of enmity; instead of death life, salvation, resurrection, heavenly treasure.

So great was the exaltation of spirit that he found in his reading of the New Testament that he wrote to his doctor son in Budapest:

1. See pp. 30–31.

From every line in the New Testament, from every word, the Jewish spirit streamed forth light, life, power, endurance, faith, hope, love, charity, limitless and indestructible faith in God, kindness to prodigality, moderation to self-denial, content to the exclusion of all sense of need, consideration for others, with extreme strictness as regards self, all these things were found pervading the book.

Almost immediately after his conversion a storm of persecution burst upon him. There was great resentment that he, a rabbi still in office, dared to testify publicly in sermons and pamphlets to the Messiahship of Jesus. Some who had been his friends scoffed at him and derided him. Others seriously warned him, pointing out the danger and the strife which would result from his conversion and his missionary activities. He was asked to remain silent about his new faith, for the sake of peace, and to keep his new ideas to himself. But, like Jeremiah of old, he felt that there was a fire in his bones, and he could not refrain from speaking: "I am in derision daily. Every one mocketh me. For since I spake, I cried out, I cried violence and spoil; because the word of the Lord was made a reproach unto me, and a derision, daily. Then I said, I will not make mention of him, nor speak any more in his name. But his word was in mine heart as a burning fire shut up in my bones, and I was weary with forbearing, and I could not stay" (Jer. 20:7–9).

In *A Jewish Mirror*, Lichtenstein he records:

I have been an honored rabbi for the space of forty years, and now, in my old age, I am treated by my friends as one possessed by an evil spirit, and by my enemies as an outcast. I am become a butt of mockers, who point the finger at me. But while I live I will stand on my watchtower though I may stand there all alone. I will listen to the words of God and look for the time when He will return to Zion in mercy, and Israel shall fill the world with his joyous cry, "Hosanna to the Son of David. . . ."

In another place, after referring to the incident of the woman afflicted for twelve years who was healed by touching the hem of Jesus' garment (Mark 5:25–35), Lichtenstein writes:

The Jew also has been sick for 2000 years, and in vain has he sought healing and help of his physicians; in vain has he spent his substance. By faith alone, and by contact with Jesus, by the power which goes forth from Jesus only can he find healing.

Lichtenstein died on October 16, 1909 at the age of 85. From the beginning he "counted the cost" of his faith, and was prepared unhesitatingly and without qualification to pay the price. Like Paul, who could boast of his Jewishness and orthodoxy, he could affirm: "What things were gain to me, those I counted loss for Christ. Yea doubtless, and I count all things but loss for the excellency of the knowledge of Christ Jesus my Lord: for whom I have suffered the loss of all things, and do count them but dung, that I may win Christ, and be found in him, not having mine own righteousness, which is of the law, but that which is through the faith of Christ, the righteousness which is of God by faith: that I may know him, and the power of his resurrection. . ." (Phil. 3:7–10).

20

*New Testament
Translator
1826–1864*

Isidor Lowenthal

ISIDOR LOWENTHAL was a man who fully exemplified the apostolic injunction to "redeem the time" (Col. 4:5). Into the space of two decades he concentrated scholarly accomplishments, linguistic attainments, and missionary achievement.

Lowenthal was born in 1826, into a German Jewish family which resided in the province of Posen. His parents made sure that he received a good education, and at the age of 17 he graduated from the Gymnasium (the equivalent of high school). As a young man, Lowenthal was involved in liberal political activities, and he was once arrested and detained by the police. In his zeal for freedom of conscience in political and religious matters he emigrated to the United States in 1846.

For a time he made a frugal living as a peddler in New York, having failed in his efforts to find better employment. But one day, while peddling his wares, he met the Rev. S. M. Gayley, of Wilmington, Delaware, who invited him to his home. Rev. Gayley took note of Lowenthal's plight and poverty, and soon discovered that he was an educated man. This so impressed him that he determined to find him a suitable position, and

127

succeeded in procuring for him an appointment as teacher of German and French in Fayette College in Easton, Pennsylvania, in 1847. Within a short time he gained proficiency in English.

For some time Lowenthal resided with Rev. Gayley and his family, and was profoundly impressed by their consistent Christian life and the godly atmosphere of their home. Their example moved him to study the New Testament. The presentation of Christ in the Gospels and in the Epistles firmly convinced him that Jesus was indeed the Messiah and the Savior of men. His conviction was expressed in public confession of his faith when he was baptized in the Presbyterian church by Rev. Gayley.

The development of his life in the purpose of God moved forward very quickly, and in 1848 he was appointed teacher of languages at Mount Holly Collegiate School. Four years later, in 1852, he entered the theological seminary at Princeton, New Jersey.

After he concluded his course he offered his services to the board of foreign missions, and in 1856 he was sent as a missionary to Afghanistan. Within a year of his arrival he had attained great facility in the native language and preached in it fluently. Unfortunately, his ministry in Afghanistan was of short duration. His life ended tragically when he was shot by his servant after only seven years in the country, when he was only 38 years of age. The shooting was said to have been accidental.

Brief though his period of missionary service proved to be, his ministry was greatly blessed of God. He translated the whole New Testament into Pushtu (the chief language of Afghanistan and some parts of India), and had the sacred volume printed. He also compiled a dictionary in Pushtu, which he left in manuscript form. He was able to preach with ease in five languages, and his knowledge of the East was second to none. His collection of Asiatic manuscripts and rare books was of great value—the largest ever possessed by a European. The people of the country held him in high regard, and he was genuinely loved by many of them, and by the European community. It may truly be said that he laid down his life in the service of Christ. Many others have benefited from the results of his scholarship and have built upon his work.

21

Musician and
Composer
1809–1847

Felix
Mendelssohn

AS LONG AS MANKIND cherishes music, the inspired compositions of Felix Mendelssohn will endure. Mendelssohn's creative genius places him in the highest rank among the most famous of the world's composers, some of whom he influenced profoundly. Indeed, it has been said that Robert Schumann, the German composer and Mendelssohn's close friend, and Anton Rubinstein, the noted pianist, studied each note of Mendelssohn's music in the hope that they might acquire something of his spirit, and embody in their compositions the facile loveliness of his music.

Much has been written about the melody, delicacy, and sensitivity of Mendelssohn's music. He had a genius for orchestration, and his compositions were "like angelic voices in remote skies." His *Midsummer Night's Dream* suite, *Fingal's Cave Overture*, the Piano Concerto in G Major, *Elijah*, and *St. Paul*, are judged to be the heights of vocal and symphonic music. So also are his *Songs Without Words*, *Walpurgis Night*, and many other works.

During the period of his musical studies Mendelssohn became deeply interested in the works of Handel and Bach, at that time little known by the general public. It was Mendelssohn who rediscovered their works, and it was his interest in Bach's music that led to the formation of a Bach Society and the publication of his masses and cantatas. Mendelssohn's performance of Bach's *St. Matthew's Passion* in Berlin, on March 11, 1829, was a significant event in the history of music.

Mendelssohn's full name was Jakob Ludwig Felix Mendelssohn-Bartholdy, and he was born on February 3, 1809 in Hamburg. His grandfather was the illustrious Jewish philosopher, Moses Mendelssohn, who led the *Haskalah*, the Jewish Renaissance Movement. Moses Mendelssohn was also the central figure in the phrase, "From Moses to Moses there was no one like Moses," the other two being the Old Testament Moses and Moses Maimonides (1135–1204, codifier of the Talmud). He was often referred to as "Moses the third," and sometimes was called "the modern Plato." Moses Mendelssohn's teachings were rejected by the orthodox Jews of his time, who felt that his ideas might incline Jews toward Christianity. Indeed, many of his followers and members of his own family did in fact become Christians. His son Abraham and his gentle cultured wife, Felix's parents, were greatly impressed by the teachings of Jesus, and had their son baptized and brought up in the Christian faith.

Mendelssohn was appropriately named Felix ("happy") since his short life—he was only 37 when he died—was an unusually happy one. All his music bears the impress of the refinement, glitter, and opulence of his environment. He was born into a family of great culture and wealth, and was cared for with tender affection from his earliest years. Only toward the end of his life did Mendelssohn know the tragedy of human helplessness and the sorrow of bereavement, when the death of his beloved sister Fanny broke his heart.

The Mendelssohn home was the meeting place for the leading intellectuals of Berlin. Goethe, Germany's leading poet, was a frequent visitor who became a friend and admirer of Felix. "I am Saul and thou art David," Goethe wrote to him. "Come to me when I am sad and discouraged, and quiet my soul with thy sweet harmonies." Felix often visited Goethe and played the piano while the grey-haired poet sat absorbed, listening to each note. The boy of ten and the aged bard understood each other deeply, and there was a close and tender bond between them.

Once, when quite overwhelmed with emotion, Goethe told his young friend, "You shall be a very great composer, Felix."

Mendelssohn's musical instruction began early in life. Both he and his sister Fanny, who was four years older, showed early signs of musical talent, and their mother gave them their first lessons. In a very short time they were ready to receive instruction from the best teachers. The boy made remarkable progress, and in the art-loving home of the Mendelssohns, musicians and artists of great prominence who lived in or passed through Berlin, gathered for the famous Sunday evening concerts which always contained some composition by the young prodigy.

In 1819, when the family had settled in Berlin, and when Felix was ten years of age, he entered the music academy there. In his eleventh year he composed a cantata and several instrumental works. When he was fifteen, in 1824, his father took him to Paris, where he met the great musician of that time, Cherubini. Cherubini heard Felix play, and predicted a great future for him. In August, 1826, Felix completed his overture to *A Midsummer Night's Dream*, and a few months later it was performed in Stettin. At about the same time his opera *The Marriage of Camacho* was performed at the Berlin Theatre.

It was at this time also that Mendelssohn began to draw public attention to Bach's music. On April 10, 1829, Felix made his London debut at a concert of the Philharmonic Society, and received the first public acknowledgment of his genius. "London worshiped him," as one reviewer wrote. Following several London concerts Mendelssohn traveled through Scotland. Later, as a result of that journey, he composed one of his most beautiful overtures, *Fingal's Cave*. During the period 1833–35 he was conductor of the musical festivals of Dusseldorf. It was in that city, in 1836, that his oratorio *St. Paul* was performed.

In 1835 Felix accepted the conductorship of the Gewandhaus Orchestra in Leipzig, and the concerts given under his leadership gained world-wide fame. Leipzig became not only the musical center of Germany but of the whole of Europe. Mendelssohn founded the Leipzig Conservatoire under the patronage of the king of Saxony, and employed on its staff a number of eminent Jewish composers. Richard Wagner, who strongly disliked Jews, complained that Leipzig was a Jewish metropolis!

Mendelssohn was married in 1837 to the widow of a pastor of the French Reformed Church. Soon after that he visited England again to conduct his oratorio *St. Paul* at the Birmingham Festival. When he returned to Leipzig he devoted all his energies to the Gewandhaus Orchestra. In 1841 he was called by the king of Prussia, Frederic William IV, to conduct a series of concerts in Berlin. In the cathedral Mendelssohn organized a body of singers which later became known as the Dome Chorus. It was while in Berlin that, in response to the wishes of the king, he composed the music to *Antigone.*

He again visited London in 1844, and conducted several concerts of the Philharmonic Society, as well as participating in various other musical events. In Birmingham he conducted the first performance of his oratorio *Elijah.* Later he gave four performances of that oratorio in various cities. Wherever he went he was warmly acclaimed for his skill and genius. Such was Mendelssohn's fame and popularity that his father once remarked: "Before, I was merely the son of my father . . . now I am the father of my son."

Mendelssohn returned to Germany from Birmingham, feeling the effects of overwork. He had never enjoyed good health, and when he heard in Frankfurt that his sister Fanny had passed away, he found the shock too great to bear. A few weeks after Fanny's death, on November 4, 1847, he passed away in Leipzig. He was buried in Trinity Cemetery in Berlin. In his brief career he produced an enormous number of compositions, seventy-two of which were published after his death. His works include operas, symphonies, cantatas, concert-overtures, concertos, chamber music, and piano and vocal pieces.

Mendelssohn was not only a great pianist, composer, and conductor; he was also a great Christian. Whereas many artists of genius—and of lesser ability—took upon themselves a license that often bordered upon licentiousness, Mendelssohn lived a life of Christian integrity which was beyond reproach. The Encyclopedia Britannica notes:

> His earnestness as a Christian needs no stronger testimony than that afforded by his own delineation of the character of St. Paul; but it is not too much to say that his heart and life were as pure as those of a little child.

In his *Dictionary of Music and Musicians,* George Grove writes:

> Few instances can be found in history of a man so amply gifted with every good quality of mind and heart; endowed with every

circumstance that would make him happy; and so thoroughly fulfilling his mission. Never perhaps could any man be found in whose life there were so few things to conceal or regret.

Some said that his expression reminded them of the Savior Himself. This was because his qualities of character, the nature of heart and mind, and his inner harmony reflected his Creator and Redeemer.

Mendelssohn served God faithfully with the wonderful gift bestowed upon him, the gift of musical genius. With the psalmist he could say, "Rejoice in the Lord, O ye righteous: for praise is comely for the upright. Praise the Lord with harp: sing unto him with psaltery and an instrument of ten strings. Sing unto him a new song; play skilfully with a loud noise" (Ps. 33:1–3). He served the Lord with gladness, and came before His presence with singing (Ps. 100), as all are enjoined to do: "Let the word of Christ dwell in you richly in all wisdom; teaching and admonishing one another in psalms and hymns and spiritual songs, singing with grace in your hearts to the Lord" (Col. 3:16).

Even in Mendelssohn's secular compositions there is a decided spiritual flavor, but it is in his sacred music that he reveals his great love and devotion to God and the things of the Spirit. His great oratorios, *Elijah* and *St. Paul,* could have been composed only by a man wholly consecrated to the God of Elijah, the most zealous of the prophets, and of St. Paul, the most zealous of the apostles. It was through Elijah that Israel recognized and acknowledged that the God of Israel was the only true God. It was through St. Paul that the message of the gospel, God's good news telling of the Messiah and Savior of mankind, was communicated to the nations so that those who were afar off might be made nigh by the blood of Christ. In his oratorios, Mendelssohn has captured and conveyed the spirit of these two faithful witnesses.

Mendelssohn's deep spiritual sense is also revealed in the music he wrote for various psalms. These are not merely modern tunes to ancient psalms. They carefully blend with the inspired words of the psalmists. Mendelssohn wrote the choruses for the psalms in the following order: Psalm 115: "Not unto us, O Lord"; Psalm 42: "As the hart panteth after the water brooks"; Psalm 95: "O come, let us sing unto the Lord"; Psalm 114: "When Israel went out of Egypt"; Psalm 2: "Why do the heathen rage"; Psalm 22: "My God, my God, why hast thou forsaken me?"; Psalm 43: "Judge me, O God, and plead my cause"; and Psalm 98: "O sing unto the Lord a new song."

Grove's *Dictionary of Music and Musicians* comments on the music set to Psalm 114:

> The Jewish blood of Mendelssohn must surely... have beat fiercely over this picture of the great triumph of his forefathers, and it is only the plain truth to say that in directness and force his music is a perfect match for the splendid words of the unknown psalmist. It is true of his oratorios also, but they have other great qualities as well.

This Jewish Christian genius gave many other sacred works to the world, and his influence on church music was profound. Many of his tunes were adapted to the words of well-known hymns, and have achieved an enduring popularity. Some examples are: "Hark, the Herald Angels Sing"; "Still, Still With Thee"; Word of God Incarnate"; "We Would See Jesus"; "Now Thank We All Our God"; and "Almighty Father, Hear Our Prayer."

Felix Mendelssohn was a Hebrew Christian who was a favorite of royal personages, great artists, and music lovers all over the world. This refutes conclusively the accusation of Jewish propagandists that a Jew who embraces the Christian faith becomes a renegade. Mendelssohn was a lover of his fellow Jews, and the friendship and help he extended to Jewish musicians often aroused the resentment of anti-Semites. But there could be no greater proof that a Jew who believes in Christ may remain a good Jew, and a credit to his people, than the fact that the Jews themselves claim Mendelssohn as their own and are proud of his Jewishness.

22

Church Historian
1789–1850

August Neander

JOHANN AUGUST WILHELM NEANDER is acknowledged as one of the most outstanding believers and among the greatest Hebrew Christians of all time. He was born David Mendel, but he changed his name when he became a Christian at the age of seventeen. David was born on January 14, 1789, in Gottingen, Germany. When he was still young his parents, who were very poor, moved to Hamburg. He received his early education in the grammer school of Hamburg, where he was an outstanding student.

While he was still a student he responded to the truth of the gospel. On February 16, 1806, he openly confessed Christ, and was baptized in the Church of St. Catherine in Hamburg. At his baptism he adopted the name Neander, meaning "new man." His new name was well chosen, and his life and witness bore eloquent witness to the fact that in Christ he was indeed a new man.

In a letter written to the pastor who had baptized him, Neander expressed the aim of his new life. He wrote:

My reception into the Holy Covenant of the higher life is to me the greatest thing for which I have to thank you, and I can only

prove my gratitude by striving to let the outward sign of baptism
into a new life become, indeed, the mark of the new life, proclaiming the reality of the new birth. . . .

Shortly after his conversion, Neander began a course of study
in Christian dogmatics at Halle, and he intended to enter the
Christian ministry. At Halle he came under the influence of the
celebrated Friedrich Ernst Schleiermacher, an independent and
speculative thinker whose ideas gained wide acceptance
among liberal and modernist theologians. But Neander was
also of an independent mind and held firm to his soundly-
based and strong convictions.

Schleiermacher's views and speculations were closely and
thoroughly examined and found wanting, and therefore had no
detrimental effect upon Neander, and his later public teaching
and pronouncements were in powerful contrast to those of his
former teacher. In a piece entitled "Memoir of the Life and
Writings of Dr. Neander," prefixed to the English translation of
Neander's *General History of the Christian Religion and
Church*, Neander's biographer refers to this period:

> It was a sad and singular sight to behold his former teacher,
> Schleiermacher, a Christian by birth, inculcating in one lecture
> room, with all the power of his mighty genius, those doctrines
> which led to the denial of the evangelical attributes of Jesus
> Christ, whilst in another room his pupil Neander, by birth a Jew,
> preached and taught salvation through faith in Christ the Son of
> God alone.

Later Neander transferred to the University of Gottingen
where he formed an association with the eminent Professor
Gottlieb Jakob Planck, at that time the leading spirit of the
famous university. During his stay at Gottingen, Neander's
capacity to probe deeply and search for original sources of
knowledge developed in keenness and power. He took nothing
for granted, and treated nothing superficially. Every factor,
every element was thoroughly examined and evaluated—for
itself and in relation to other details. This characteristic has
made his literary work highly valuable.

On completing his university studies with distinction Neander was accepted for the work of the ministry. It soon became
clear to him, however, that his life was to be devoted to
scholarship. Not the church, but the college hall; not the pulpit,

but the professorial chair, were to constitute his sphere of life and service. Thus, after a brief engagement as tutor at Heidelberg in 1810, he took his place among the distinguished professors at the University of Berlin as Professor of Church History. Among his tutorial colleagues was his former teacher Friedrich Schleiermacher, as well as the distinguished Professor Wilhelm Martin De Wette.

In his academic work he was, throughout his life, a most painstaking, industrious, and masterly professor. In addition, he was a prolific writer and a recognized author. His was industrious in his application to study and teaching. He never married and so was able to devote his time and energies exclusively to his calling as a scholar, writer, and lecturer. Because he was never ordained he never preached in the formal sense, but in his lectures he took the opportunity to teach Christian truth in its practical, doctrinal, and historical applications.

In rapid succession he produced volume after volume, all the product of deep study and devoted labor. His *Life of Christ; History of the Planting and the Training of the Christian Church by the Apostles:* and especially the many volumes of his great work, *The General History of the Christian Religion and Church,* made his name familiar to and respected by Christian leaders and students.

Partly due to the popularity of his writings, his classroom was always crowded. His lectures were attended not only by undergraduates and students but also by professors of his own and other universities. Protestants and Roman Catholics alike sat at his feet. Usually he gave three lectures each day on different subjects. It could fairly be said that he was at once the most popular, most respected, and most beloved professor of the University of Berlin during the first half-century of its existence. Although at that time it was the youngest of German universities, it rapidly achieved the foremost rank in the teaching of science and literature, through highly gifted professors such as Friedrich Schleiermacher, Johann Fichte, Georg Hegel, Friedrich von Schelling, Karl Lachmann, Franz Bopp, and Heinrich Ritter. Of Neander, Julian Schmidt wrote:

> There was in the otherwise almost comical appearance of this man something peculiarly lovable, a purity and simplicity, a childlikeness in regard to all worldly things, an unreserved surrender to the holiest, so that he passed as with closed eyes

through the streets of the capital and through the turmoil of theological disputes.

But Neander did not separate himself from worldly affairs and events. He was keenly alive to all that went on around him. And he was concerned for people. Each one found in him what he most needed—comfort, warning, or encouragement. Many visited him in his home, and received spiritual help and instruction. His students looked upon him as a father in God, and as a counselor always ready to give—but never force—his advice wherever it was sought.

No needy person ever appealed to him in vain for aid. His charity and generosity were unbounded. His own wants were few and modest, and he gave the bulk of his income to others. The proceeds from the sale of his numerous works were devoted to philanthropic and missionary purposes. If he were short of money at any time, he would take a valuable book and pawn it, so that he might have something to give to any needy person who appealed to him. Consequently, he was beloved for his kindness of heart and his gentleness, and was widely respected for his scholarship and teaching ability. His place of abode was a true home, and he shared it with his sister. It was a favorite meeting place both for his students and for professors and preachers, such as Strauss, Schelling, Ritter, Ranke, and Krummacher.

From the glimpses his visitors gained of his private life, many learned what it means to belong to Christ. He showed many the way of salvation. To him, Christian truth was no mere system of theology. It was a new life, initiated and sustained by the saving power of God. Christ was the ideal of his life; the constant theme of his conversation, and he took every opportunity to speak to his friends of Him "from whom all good gifts come and who has promised ever to be near to the broken and the contrite heart."

Christ was also the invariable theme of his letters to his friends. To one of his friends he wrote:

God so loved you that He gave His only begotten Son for you, that you might have the eternal life which is for you an unquestionable certainty. He has not spared His own Son, but delivered Him up for you, and shall he not with Him freely give you all things? Who shall lay anything to your charge since God in

Christ has justified you? Who shall condemn you since Christ has died for you and is ever at the right hand of God, making intercession for you? These are not my words but the words of the Almighty God spoken directly to you in His Holy Scriptures.

Neander's words and actions were always regulated by the precepts of his Master, and he was ever ready publicly to support the cause of Christ and to openly testify for his Master and Lord.

But the supreme object of his life, as a scholar and author, was to prepare a comprehensive history of Christianity and the church. This was produced under the title *A General History of the Christian Religion and Church*, and in the preface to the first edition, Neander declared his purpose: "To exhibit the history of the church of Christ as a living witness to the divine power of Christianity, as a school of Christian experience, a voice sounding through the ages, of instruction, of doctrine and of reproof, for all who are disposed to listen."

Neander was not the historian of a dead past. He regarded the past as the continuing and developing movement of history toward a predestined end. To him the past was the beginning of a greater present and the preparation for a more glorious future; the past was the foundation of the building of the church throughout the ages. Neander had implicit faith in the abiding presence of Christ in his church, and of its consequent power to influence and transform the world.

In his history Neander traced in detail the process of church development over the centuries—a process of steady and irresistible growth and progress, despite all attempts to hinder it. Christianity is a divine power manifested and operative from heaven at the incarnation of Christ, and giving a new quality and character to the life of the human race.

In defining and describing the action in history of that power, Neander's pen was ever active, and in addition to his three outstanding works mentioned Neander also wrote: *Anti Gnosticus; Development of the Gnostic System;* biographies of Julian the Apostate, St. Bernard, and St. Chrysostom; *Unity and Variety of the Christian Life; Memorabilia from the History of the Christian Life; Memoirs of the Proceedings of the Berlin Royal Academy of Sciences;* and numerous essays contributed to various religious periodicals.

Neander knew the power of the printed word, and to further

the interests and aims of the Prussian Bible Society he gave many important lectures. In addition, he was a staunch supporter of foreign missions and of all philanthropic undertakings. Through his literature, his lectures, and his life he strongly influenced a great number of students who later became ministers in town and country charges, where they faithfully instructed their congregations in the simple gospel of God's grace.

Christianity owes an immense debt of gratitude to Neander for his defense of "the faith once delivered to the saints" in its fundamental integrity. He held back for a time the tide of rationalism, skepticism, and infidelity which threatened to engulf not only Germany but the whole of Christendom. He was called upon expressly to remedy the harm perpetrated by the speculative teaching of Dr. David Friedrich Strauss who had written a life of Christ (*Das Leben Jesu, Kritisch Bearbeitet,* 1835–36), which questioned many of the fundamental facts of the gospel story. The forceful argument of Strauss's thesis spread doubt even among Christians, and the various translations of *Das Leben Jesu* brought its influence to most European countries.

The godly king of Prussia was greatly concerned by the appearance of the book, and contemplated the issue of an order prohibiting its circulation. He consulted Neander, however, who advised, "If intellectual weapons are used against the truth then the same weapons should be used in its vindication." The king thereupon suggested that Neander write his own life of Christ. As a result of Neander's publication, Strauss's position was shattered and his book passed into oblivion.

In his declining years Neander was almost totally blind, but he was confident that his affliction was within the will of God for him, and was willing for His will. Neander did not, however, allow his failing vision to hinder his work for his Master. So devoted was he that there is little doubt his earnest activities shortened his life. Indeed, on the last day of his life he insisted on dictating the closing pages of his church history, and it is recorded that in the evening of that day he said to his sister, "I am weary. Come, let us go home." Shortly after reaching his home he passed to the dwelling place prepared by His Lord for His servants, to dwell for ever in His presence. His pilgrimage ended on July 14, 1850, in his sixty-second year, and he was buried in the Jerusalem Churchyard in Berlin.

The imposing funeral cortege was honored by the presence of royal personages and numerous government officials, and included clergymen, professors, and students of the universities of Halle and Berlin. Crowds thronged the entire route from Neander's home to the cemetery, a distance of two miles, and many watched from windows and doorways. Neander's Bible and Greek Testament were carried before the hearse as a testimony to one who had done so much to keep alight in Germany the torch of pure and undiluted Christianity.

His life and work were summed up in the *Living Age* of January, 1851:

> In the death of Neander, Germany has lost one of her greatest teachers, and the Christian world one of its greatest ornaments. A purer and nobler character has seldom adorned any church— one in which the loftiest powers of nature and the lowliest graces of the Gospel were finely blended, and which more fixed, therefore, at once the love and the admiration of all who came in contact with it.

When Neander was buried, funeral orations were preached by several great men of Berlin, including Dr. Friedrich Krummacher, who described Neander as "one of the noblest of the noble in the kingdom of God, the youngest of the fathers of the church, of whom it might be said, as of the apostle John, 'This disciple shall not die.' "

23

*Representative of the
Lutheran Church
1809–1882*

Friedrich Adolph Philippi

THE FAMILY environment into which Friedrich Adolph Philippi was born was one of security and tradition. His father was a Berlin banker, and the Jewish laws and customs were faithfully observed in his household. But the general intellectual and religious situation was one of fluidity, speculation and investigation. Friedrich's family was not unresponsive to the new liberalism in theology. When Friedrich was born in 1809, the "enlightenment movement" was widely influential, and especially so in Germany. It was also somewhat disruptive.

Friedrich's parents, under the influence of the movement, sent their boy to a public school instead of to the usual Jewish school. The family's break with orthodoxy is not surprising, for the strong enlightenment movement, known in Hebrew as *haskalah*, appeared at the end of the eighteenth century to oppose Jewish ghettoism and to encourage the adoption of the culture and manners of the peoples among which the Jews lived. The movement emphasized the study of biblical Hebrew and scientific literature rather than the Talmud.

It was at school that Friedrich learned something of the Christian faith and heard of Jesus. To him this was new knowledge, and it made a deep impression upon him. This impression was intensified during the tercentenary celebrations of the Reformation in 1817. In his thirteenth year, Philippi entered the Gymnasium, or high school, where Christian influence worked still more strongly upon him. This and other factors ultimately led him to faith in Christ.

One of the teachers at the school, who gave him private tuition in mathematics, was a Jewish Christian named Herr Jacobi. Friedrich had often heard at home that a Jew who becomes a Christian does so not from personal conviction but for ulterior motives, and he mentioned this to his teacher. But Jacobi was able to convince Friedrich that he had become a Christian because he truly believed Jesus was the Savior of the world. The teacher wisely urged Friedrich to read and study the New Testament and thus learn firsthand the truth about Jesus.

At that time a book entitled *Glockenton (Chimes)* by Dr. Strauss had aroused great interest and attention, and was widely discussed. Its aim was to counteract the growing and destructive influence of agnosticism, and the book had a powerful effect on Friedrich. He therefore went frequently to hear Dr. Strauss preach, and it was to him that Philippi expressed his desire to become a Christian.

The experienced pastor warned Friedrich not to be too hasty in making his decision, and advised him that at his age he should consult with his parents before taking such a serious step. He was then only fifteen years old and knew beyond any doubt that his parents would never approve of his conversion. He also knew that if he became a Christian he would be disinherited.

When he was 18, after a period of unrest due to his unwillingness to make the sacrifices that a decision for Christ would involve, Friedrich entered the University of Berlin. Here he studied philology, and in 1830 took his degree as Doctor of Philosophy. At the university he attended theological lectures given by August Neander (see chap. 22) and these, as well as the quality and integrity of Neander's life, further impressed him with the validity of the truth as it is in Jesus.

After a distressing and painful inner struggle Philippi finally decided to accept the Savior's invitation to "Come unto me, all ye that labour and are heavy laden, and I will give you rest" (Matt. 11:28). On the day after Christmas, 1829, he made a public confession of faith in Christ and was baptized. When his parents heard of his baptism he was, as he himself expressed it, "cut off from the circle of his nearest and dearest."

After his baptism Philippi served for some years as a teacher in Dresden and Berlin. In 1837 he began to give lectures on theological subjects at the University of Berlin. Ten years later he accepted a professorship at the University of Dorpat, where he exercised a strong and productive influence over the students, convincing them that "Christ is the end of the law for righteousness to every one that believeth."

While at Dorpat, Philippi participated effectively in the struggle of the Lutherans against the encroachments of the Russian church. In 1851 he left Dorpat on accepting a call to Rostock, where he boldly championed the cause of Christian truth against the influences of rationalism. His book, *The Teaching of Faith*, did much to create a deep and enduring respect for the Lutheran creed among other churches, a service which was heartily appreciated by all branches of the Lutheran church in Germany, the Scandinavian countries, and in Russia.

For many years Professor Philippi was afflicted with heart weakness, and on August 29, 1882, at the age of 73, he passed into the presence of the Lord. His last words were: "How beautiful! How beautiful! Have mercy!"

In his biography Ludwig Schultze says of Philippi:

Philippi was called out of Israel by God to be a witness to the church. He was at home in science, poetry, and the wisdom of this world, yet held all in subservience to that which is highest. Refusing professorships in Bonn and Erlangen he chose to serve the millions of Lutherans from Rostock. The extent to which his life-work was appreciated is evidenced by the recognition he received on his fiftieth anniversary, when his Alma Mater bestowed upon him his philosophical degree. The city council of Rostock honored him with the gold medal for art and science, and tributes of the highest esteem poured in upon him from the faculties of Berlin, Dorpat, Leipzig, Christiana, and Upsala.

The Lutheran Cyclopedia comments:

If Dorpat and Rostock are even today strongholds of sound Lutheranism, and if the church in the Baltic provinces and in the province of Mecklenburg is firm in its Lutheran faith, these conditions are in large measure due to the fullness of faith and the vigorous personality that characterized Philippi. Professor Frank of Erlangen said of him: "The church which has such a teacher as the educator of its ministers must be counted fortunate."

24

Jewish Leader
1837–1899

Joseph Rabinowitz

LIKE MANY Hebrew Christians, Joseph Rabinowitz owed his conversion to the reading of the New Testament. His experience was a verification of God's promise to the people of Israel, "My word . . . shall not return unto me void, but it shall accomplish that which I please, and it shall prosper in the thing whereto I sent it" (Isa. 55:11).

Joseph Rabinowitz was a Russian Jew whose father, David ben Ephraim, was a member of a Chassidic-rabbinic family. Joseph was born in Resina, a town on the River Dneister in Southern Russia, on September 23, 1837. His mother died when he was quite young, and until he was eleven years of age he was cared for by her father, Nathan Neta, in the town of Orgeyev. He was afterward cared for by other relatives.

At the age of thirteen, when he was bar mitzva, Joseph was betrothed, in accordance with Jewish custom at that time. In those days the government required all children to learn the Russian language. By so doing, Joseph became acquainted with non-Jewish literature. An entirely new world was opened to him, a world completely different from what he had learned about in the Hebrew books he had studied. When he was eighteen years old he received a copy of the Hebrew New Testament which, according to *The History of the London Society for Promoting Christianity Among the Jews,* was sent to him by one of the society's missionaries. (However, some of Joseph's biographers claim that he received the New Testament from his brother-in-law.)

The first effect of his reading of the New Testament was that he began to question the traditions of Judaism accepted and observed among the Jews. At that time he returned to his grandfather in Orgeyev, and devoted his time to the study of the Bible. He also learned Russian Law in order to become a solicitor working among his people. It was at this stage in his life, in 1856, that he married.

His interest and involvement in the welfare of the local Jewish community developed into a strong concern for the well-being of the whole of Russian Jewry. He was especially interested in the education of Jewish children. Intellectually he was a progressive thinker, and he propagated his ideas for the reform and modernization of Jewish life by giving lectures in his home town of Kischeneff, where there was a large Jewish community. Many of his lectures were published in the Jewish press. In 1878 he wrote an article for the Hebrew paper *Haboker Or* in which he urged the rabbis to contribute toward the improvement of the lot of Russian Jews by teaching them the importance of becoming an agricultural people.

Severe persecution of the Jews broke out in 1882. The situation of Russian Jewry was desperate, and Rabinowitz began to consider the idea of the Jews emigrating to Palestine. With a view to establishing a Jewish colony, he went to Palestine on a mission of inquiry. While he was there he studied the land, and became acquainted with the temporal and spiritual condition of the Jewish community. In his travels and inquiries he derived great help from the New Testament descriptions of historic places and events of biblical import. In his reading and study he was deeply impressed by the personality of Jesus, and began seriously to consider the validity of His claim to be the true Messiah.

Unfortunately, he found conditions in Palestine disappointing and frustrating. Indeed, he was heartbroken, and decided to return home. Before leaving, however, he climbed the Mount of Olives. When he reached the summit and looked down upon the city of Jerusalem he became deeply reflective, and asked himself, "Why has the City of David been desolate for so many centuries? Why are my people scattered abroad over all the earth? Why these recurrent persecutions?"

As his mind dwelt on these questions his gaze turned toward Golgotha, where Jesus was crucified. As he looked upon the sacred spot he recalled the words of Isaiah 53, and compared them with the sufferings of Jesus. In that moment he realized that beyond a shadow of a doubt Jesus was indeed the promised Messiah who gave His life for His people. Later he explained, "Now I saw the answers to my questions. We had rejected the Messiah. Therefore were we scattered. Therefore were we persecuted and could find no rest."

His reflections strengthened his conviction that Jesus was his personal Redeemer and King, as well as Lord of all. Opening the New Testament, his glance fell on the words of John 15:5, "I am the vine, ye are the branches . . . without me ye can do nothing." As he read the entire chapter he saw "clearly that our Jewish millionaires cannot help us; that our colonies in Palestine are useless. Our only hope lies in our brother Jesus, whom we have crucified, but whom God has raised up and set on His own right hand on high." Rabinowitz returned to Russia with the following report: "The key to the Holy Land is in the hands of our brother Jesus. If His words would take root in our hearts they would bring forth the fruits of righteousness and peace."

This idea he made the ideal, the principle, and the basis of all his future work. He drew up a list of thirteen articles of faith and labor, after the pattern of the thirteen Principles of Faith set down by Moses Maimonides. The substance of the articles was that Jesus is the only Savior of Israel, as well as of the whole world. With great courage, and in the face of bitter opposition, he endeavored to promulgate his convictions. With tact and love he overcame much of the opposition, and gained supporters in Kischeneff and other towns in Bessarabia. He began what was referred to as the Rabinowitz Movement.

Rabinowitz's followers were called "Israelites of the New Covenant," and in 1885 he published his *Symbols of the Israelites of the New Covenant* in seven articles. He was greatly encouraged by Professor Franz Delitzsch, the translator of the New Testament into Hebrew, and by Rev. John Wilkinson, the founder of the Mildmay Mission to the Jews. In Glasgow, Scotland an association was formed in 1887 for the support of his work.

Rabinowitz was baptized in Berlin by Professor Mead of Andover, Massachusetts on March 22, 1885, and he was asked by the pastor of the Lutheran church at Kischeneff to join the church. He declined, however, for neither he nor his followers, who had separated from the synagogue, could worship in a church where there was a crucifix. For yet stronger reasons he could not join the Russian church, though he was asked to do so by its highest authorities.

Instead, Rabinowitz built a hall where he faithfully and clearly preached the gospel of God's grace. His eloquent sermons were clearly illustrated by parables, after the pattern of Christ's own sermons, and the methods of Russian and East European Chassidim and rabbis. One example is the parable called *The Lost Wheel*:

> Two foolish people were traveling in a four-wheeled wagon. Noticing that the wagon moved heavily, they examined it, and found that a wheel was missing. One of the foolish people sprang out, and ran forward along the road, saying to every one he met, "We have lost a wheel. Have you seen one?" At last a wise man said to him, "You are looking in the wrong direction! You should seek your wheel behind the wagon, not in front of it."
>
> This is the mistake which the Jews have been making all these centuries. They have been looking forward instead of backward. It may be said that the four wheels of Hebrew history are Abraham, Moses, David, and Jesus. The Jews have been looking into the future when they should have been looking into the past. This is why they have not found their fourth wheel.
>
> But God be thanked that the sons of the New Covenant (Jer. 33:31; Heb. 8:8) have found Jesus, that most important wheel of all. Abraham, Moses, and David are, after all, only types and forerunners of Jesus. Thank God, we have found our brother Jesus, our all in all, who is made unto us wisdom and righteousness, and sanctification and redemption (I Cor. 1:30); in whom alone we have found light and life, liberty and love, both for the great present and for the still greater hereafter. And now we look with longing eyes and joyful hearts towards the brightness of His appearing.

Soon after Joseph's baptism, his wife and seven children, his brother and his family, and several other Jews who heard the gospel from his lips publicly confessed Christ as their Savior. In addition, the attitude of the Jews in general toward the person of Christ softened somewhat. But it was not only through his preaching and speaking that Jews were won. Through Rabinowitz's published sermons and other writings which were scattered widely throughout Russia, a great number of Jews were led to Christ. This was the beginning of the Hebrew Christian novement in Russia.

At the age of 62 Rabinowitz died, exhausted by his labors.

25

Minister, Missionary,
and Bible Teacher
1876–1931

Shabbetai Benjamin Rohold

SHABBETAI BENJAMIN ROHOLD was born in Jerusalem on February 20, 1876. He had a "goodly heritage." His grandfather, Moses Baruch, was a rabbi of distinction. His father, Naphtali, was a respected Palestinian rabbi who ministered in Jerusalem. With such a distinguished family background, Shabbetai naturally received the best rabbinical education available in the Holy City, and he became a proficient Talmudic scholar.

His father was more progressive than many of his Jewish contemporaries, and he sought to give his children a broader secular education than was the custom among the Jews. He hired a German tutor to instruct them in the German language, and in the subjects generally taught in Gentile schools. But Naphtali Rohold was also a cautious man, and he was careful to instruct the tutor, who was a Christian, not to impart Christian ideas to the Rohold children.

However, the Old Testament was used in the school as a textbook for translation exercises, and Shabbetai one day read the fifty-third chapter of Isaiah. He was puzzled by its content and intent, and, although he vaguely guessed to whom it referred, he dared not to discuss the matter with anyone. But God was working all things together for good, and even the ordinary events of his life combined to lead him nearer to the truth.

From time to time, with a few companions bent on mischief, Shabbetai would play tricks on an old missionary who lived in the neighborhood, and whom the Jewish boys considered fair game. But the old man never lost his temper or rebuked them. Instead, he treated the boys with kindness and patience. He even invited them to visit him in his home. Eventually they responded, and thereafter became frequent visitors. Soon they were involved in discussing passages in the Old Testament which refer to the promised Messiah. Rohold was deeply impressed by the character of the missionary, and by what seemed to be his strange interpretation of the Messianic scriptures. But further careful perusal of the Old Testament prophecies led him to an inner acknowledgment that Jesus of Nazareth was the one of whom Moses and the prophets wrote and spoke.

Nevertheless, years of mental and spiritual conflict passed before he dared to make a public confession of his new faith. His final decision was a heartbreaking experience. From the Jewish point of view it meant bringing disgrace on families: the breaking of family ties; the deprivation of a loving, comfortable home; the frustration, or abandonment, of all the hopes and plans which had hitherto directed his life. It meant the loss of all things that were near and dear to him.

But, by the grace of God, Rohold was able to count the cost, and to pay it for Christ's sake. He surmounted all obstacles and temptations to shirk the sacrifice and the surrender. As he writes of his experience:

> God called upon me in the Holy City, Jerusalem, to forsake all and follow Him. It was His wonderful grace, abiding mercy, and matchless love that enabled me to leave all—home, nearest, dearest, and best—and to take up the cross and follow Jesus. He became my Savior, Redeemer, Master, friend, and the source of my hopes, my peace, my joy and consolation. All these years He, the all-sufficient Father, has led me and I have followed in a childlike faith and complete trust.

On December 21, 1898, at the age of twenty-three, Benjamin Rohold was publicly admitted to the membership of the Christian church, when he was living in the Stepney district of London. Nine months later he was appointed superintendent of the Bonar Memorial Mission to the Jews in Glasgow, Scotland.

In his new position, Dr. Rohold worked among the Jews of Glasgow as a trainee or student missionary. By his patience and steadfastness, he gradually won the confidence of the Jewish community, many of whom were accustomed to regard the Jewish missionary as a renegade and a traitor to his people. By his tact and Jewish learning, and by his help as occasional mediator between immigrant Jews and their Scottish neighbors, he gained a place of true regard among both communities.

During this period he completed the full course at the Bible Training Institute of Glasgow, and took classes at the university and at what is now Trinity College. He thus added to his specifically Jewish learning the training necessary for the position of a Christian minister. His intellectual and spiritual abilities and both kinds of training gained him a welcome in the homes of leading thinkers in Glasgow, and many lifelong friendships were formed.

Dr. Rohold's reputation spread beyond the borders of Scotland, and in 1908 he accepted an invitation from the Presbyterian church in Canada. For nearly thirteen years he labored among the Jews of Toronto, and the work for Israel's redemption there begun soon had branches all over Canada. He was ordained in 1909 as a Presbyterian minister. In Toronto he met and married Belle Petrie, a voluntary worker in the mission.

Two outstanding results of his work and influence were the opening of the Christian Synagogue in June, 1913 and the formation of the Hebrew Christian Alliance in 1914. Dr. Rohold was elected first president of the Alliance and later became the first editor of *The Hebrew Christian Alliance Quarterly*.

No account of Dr. Rohold's work in Canada could in any way equal the recognition recorded in the minutes of the Presbytery on the occasion of Dr. Rohold's departure to take up work in Palestine:

In accepting the resignation of the Rev. S. B. Rohold, the Presbytery desires to put on record its deep sense of the loss we suffer in dissolving the tie which has bound Mr. Rohold to us, and to the Jewish mission for almost thirteen crowded years. [He has given] faithful, earnest, successful and, we venture to think, unique service on behalf of Israel at Toronto, and other points in Canada. The Presbytery recognizes the task of evangelizing Israel to be one of the great importance and urgency, but also . . . one of unusual complexity, delicacy, and difficulty. We therefore heartily record our appreciation of the remarkable success which has attended the ministry of Mr. Rohold in organizing the mission, disarming prejudices among both Jews and Gentiles, commanding the respect of all, enlisting the sympathy and cooperation of many Christians, [and] winning many Jews. [We are indebted to him for] conceiving, establishing, and, through meritorious service, building up the Hebrew Christian Synagogue, the solitary institution of its kind in America.

As we ponder our loss through the departure of Mr. and Mrs. Rohold, we are somewhat comforted by the reflection that the service to which Mr. Rohold is called is the very front trenches of Jewish evangelization and one for which his birth, talents, culture, and wide experience peculiarly fit him.

In 1921, Dr. Rohold took charge of the B. J. S. Mission[1] at the foot of Mt. Carmel in Haifa. The mission was the Palestinian station of the British Society for the Propagation of the Gospel Among the Jews, and Dr. Rohold proved to be the right man for the position. He was of Palestinian birth, spoke the languages of the country fluently, understood the ways of life of the various peoples, and had the confidence of all citizens, as well as of the Christian church.

Nevertheless, the start of his work was far from easy. World War I had caused deterioration and destruction to the mission property, and Dr. and Mrs. Rohold had to live for many months in two desolate cellar rooms. They faced many discomforts and difficulties daily. But they slowly overcame their problems, and by faith, patience, and perseverance, Dr. Rohold built up a remarkable, highly effective work. Mrs. Rohold was a constant and capable support to her husband. She was his equal in zeal and service, and after his death in 1931, continued to supervise the work until her death in 1960.

A medical clinic for outpatients was established and proved a valuable means of contact with both Jews and Arabs. A reading room was opened where literature was supplied to visitors, and inquirers were dealt with. This led to the recognition of the mission as the center for the distribution of Christian literature for the leading missions in Palestine and the surrounding countries. Mrs. Rohold initiated and maintained a work among women and children, and a great many were influenced by the classes she conducted with the aid of competent teachers and assistants.

1. British Jew Society Mission

The mission conducted Sabbath schools, Sunday schools, Bible classes, and services for all groups in the community in four different languages. Mr. Rohold was a prolific writer and was the author of many tracts for Jews and pamphlets for Christians. He wrote hundreds of articles on Judaism for leading magazines and periodicals. He was a fine scholar, well-versed in Talmudical literature and in Jewish life.

In the last two years of his life Dr. Rohold became gravely ill, and in January, 1931 he entered a sanatorium in Egypt to escape the inclement weather in Haifa. But his condition worsened. After only ten years of substantial labor in Palestine he was called to a higher service. He died on February 14, 1931, and was buried in the British Protestant cemetery in Old Cairo.

Dr. Rohold's friend and associate, Rev. Dr. W. M. Christie, gave tribute:

> The services of Mr. Rohold were not limited either to the mission in Haifa or to Haifa. He took a great interest in, and had a share in, the establishing on Mt. Carmel of an annual summer conference for the deepening of spiritual life among Greek priests. He had the full confidence of the Greek church authorities, and on the occasion of a dispute among the villagers of their communion he was called upon to act as mediator. So satisfactorily was the work carried through that the Patriarchate conferred on him the Knighthood of the Grand Cross and Star of the Holy Sepulchre. In like manner he brought about peace on another occasion between Druse and Moslem villagers.
>
> In addition to the practically unique honor mentioned, it is worthy of note that Mr. Rohold was welcomed as a Fellow or member into quite a number of learned societies. His literary work too, was of a high order. His sermons in Yiddish and Hebrew have already had wide circulation, and his contributions to the missionary and magazine press have brought illumination to many who had hitherto known only Gentile darkness of things Jewish.
>
> Gifted with great powers of organization, and the ability to fix upon essentials, coupled with an understanding of those with whom he had to deal, he invariably reached the goal in view. Those he gathered around him were rather friends than employees, and of them and their comfort he was ever careful. Responsive to such treatment they rendered him loyal, genuine service. The more he was understood, the better he was appreciated and the more he was loved. And the secret of it all was that there was a constant "correspondence with heaven." From the day of his conversion in April, 1895, till the Homecall he stood by the written Word, faithful to its teaching; and the living Word that came down from heaven stood by him, for his anchor was cast at Calvary.

The tribute was well deserved. He had served his Lord as a missionary among the Jews for thirty-three years, and was the means of winning many Jewish souls for Christ. He was zealous in his activities to disseminate the good tidings among his fellow Jews. Yet he was always unassuming in his manner, courteous, and gentlemanly in all his relationships with his fellowmen.

26

Hebraist, Translator,
and Missionary
1820–1883

Isaac Salkinson

ISAAC SALKINSON, like many other outstanding and scholarly Hebrew Christians, was a Russian Jew. He came from what could then be called the "reservoir" of Jewish orthodoxy, East European Jewry. He was born in Vilna, which was the Lithuanian capital until Lithuania was added to Russia in 1795. It was the ninth largest town in Imperial Russia, and its population of about 197,000 was mostly Jewish. The date of Salkinson's birth is not known. His father died when Isaac was only four years old, and his mother died a few years later. Little is known of his family background or of his boyhood, but it is established that his strictly orthodox parents wanted him to become a rabbi. In his youth he had the same idea and intention. To that end he diligently prepared himself, and planned to emigrate to American in order to enter a rabbinical seminary for the necessary training.

But the God of Israel had His own purpose for Isaac Salkinson, who was led first to London, where he was brought into touch with Christian missionaries who made known to him the "gospel of God concerning His Son Jesus Christ our Lord." Salkinson was so irresistibly attracted by the story of Christ that, comparing the record of Jesus' life with Old Testament prophecies, he was unshakably convinced that the Jesus of the New Testament was the Messiah promised in the Old Testament. Without hesitation he openly confessed his faith in Christ and was baptized.

In order to prepare himself for missionary work among his own people, Salkinson entered the London College of the British Society for the Propagation of the Gospel Among the Jews. On the completion of his course he was appointed to work as a Jewish missionary in Scotland, under the auspices of the United Presbyterian church. At the same time he became a student at Divinity Hall in Edinburgh, and in 1859 was ordained to the Presbyterian ministry, and served the church in Glasgow.

Very little is known of Salkinson's private life. Who took care of him when he was orphaned as a very young child is not recorded. Nor are the dates of his arrival in England and his journey to the United States. Little is known about his wife, for though he often spoke of her as his invaluable helpmate in his missionary work, no biographical details of her appear. In 1864 Salkinson resumed his work with the British Society as missionary to his Jewish brethren, and labored in the gospel in various cities and towns throughout Europe. Twelve months later he settled in Vienna, where he worked until his death on June 5, 1883, at the age of about 60 years.

Isaac Salkinson greatly distinguished himself as a linguist. At the age of four he was already able to read the Old Testament in the original Hebrew, and throughout his life he exercised his linguistic gifts, especially in the translation of standard works into Hebrew. In his natural modesty he referred to Hebrew translation as "the only talent" given to him, but it is known that he was greatly gifted in his work as minister and missionary.

In the year prior to this ordination, Salkinson published his Hebrew version of *The Philosophy of the Plan of Salvation*, which had excited considerable attention. His translation was highly praised by principal Professor Davidson, his former tutor and friend in the British Society's Jewish Mission College, and who judged that the volume might be valuable for circulation among the Jews. Davidson's high opinion of the book carried much weight with Salkinson, and it was this that stimulated him to translate the work in the first place. The translation was published under the Hebrew title *SOD ha-JESHUA (The Mystery of Salvation)*. Professor Davidson wrote:

> Mr. Salkinson is justly deserving of the grateful encouragement of the spiritual friends of Israel; and while praying for a blessing to accompany the distribution of his work and his own personal labor among his brethren according to the flesh, we can but wish that he may feel induced to serve his generation by additional productions of many more of the like useful works.

Encouraged by the success of this translation, Salkinson translated into Hebrew John Milton's *Paradise Lost*, which was published in Vienna in 1870. Of this translation the Rev. J. J. Steward Perowne, Dean of Peterborough, commented:

> I have examined many portions of the translation, and especially those in which there is reference to the divinity of the Messiah, and I have no hesitation in saying that the translator has rendered the work faithfully. I think he has shown considerable skill in triumphing over the difficulty of an adequate rendering of Milton's theological expressions.

Among eminent clergymen, the Rev. J. R. Lumby, Professor of Divinity at Cambridge, also wrote:

> I have looked over with some care several long passages of Mr. Salkinson's translation into Hebrew of Milton's *Paradise Lost*, and have been astonished with the closeness of the version which he has made, and the wonderful power, which is everywhere shown in it, of clothing the sense of the English in the diction borrowed almost entirely from the Hebrew Scriptures. With the purpose of testing the fidelity of Mr. Salkinson's version in those parts of the poem which speak expressly of the divinity and office of our Savior, I selected the Third Book for special examination. As a whole he has produced a version which sets forth Christian teaching almost as definitely as does the Apostles' Creed.

This work was followed by his translation of Shakespeare's *Othello*, published in Vienna in 1874, with a preface by Perez Smolensky, one of the best known Hebrew writers and editors of the day. Four years later Salkinson published his translation of *Romeo and Juliet*, and Tiedge's *Urania*, a Christian poetical work which is highly valued by the Jewish people.

His translations did not distract him from his regular work as a missionary to the Jews, for he said, "My missionary work consists in personal intercourse with my brethren, in corresponding with them, and especially in writing treatises in Hebrew on their behalf."

Dr. Salkinson's ideas on the differences between Jews and Gentiles as missionaries to the Jews reveal his insight and wisdom:

> As to the assertion that a Gentile missionary is the most acceptable to the Jews, I would say, certainly he has, among others, two important advantages. There is no personal enmity against him, and he will not be reasonably suspected of being insincere in his own faith. Consequently, the motive in his effort to convert the Jew will not be wrongly construed. Not so the Jewish missionary. At his first appearance the thoughts of the Jew are like the following: "Here is one who brought shame upon his parents, betrayed the national faith, rebelled against God; and this great sin is light to him, so that he now seeks to cause Israel to sin."
>
> Then, again, measuring others with themselves, they suppose it is impossible for a Jew ever to become a true believer in the Savior of the Gentiles; hence the missionary is regarded as a hypocrite, given to filthy lucre. Nevertheless, this disadvantage is evanescent, or rather is overruled for the best, when in the course of time, by his walk and conversation, he is recognized as a true believer in the faithful follower of the Lord Jesus; then his example has great weight, which the Gentile's has not.
>
> Again, the Gentile may start with sincere love to the Jew, but when he happens to be cheated by one vagabond Jew, disappointed in another, and ill-treated by a third, his love to the nation will soon cool, though he may remain firm on the side of the Master. Not so the converted Jew. If he possess native patriotism at all he is as strong as death; all the waters of affliction cannot quench the fire of his love.
>
> Now, leaving out other considerations, let me express my long-cherished opinion, strengthened by experience, that the best way would be to couple the Gentile with the Jew, so that the two may make one complete missionary—provided only that they previously knew each other well and found their minds homogenical, so that they may not be unequally yoked together. . . . In this way alone, I believe, can the Gentile missionary be of great service, but I would never advise him to go alone.

But Salkinson's greatest work was his Hebrew translation of the Greek New Testament under the title *Ha 'Brith-ha' Chadashah (The New Covenant)*. After Salkinson was engaged by the British Society Committee to produce a new Hebrew version of the New Testament, he wrote:

I undertook the work with delight, the more so since many learned Jews repeatedly expressed to me their astonishment that I had not undertaken it long ago. When the work is published it will be seen that my labors as a Jewish missionary have not been in vain in the Lord.

When for the first time in my life I read the New Testament, it was a Hebrew version. I felt then how great a necessity there was for a version in idiomatic Hebrew. This I could do now since I have acquired a knowledge of reading the New Testament in its original Greek.

The translation was undertaken for the British Society in 1881, and was published posthumously under the supervision of Dr. C. D. Ginsburg in Vienna, in 1886. When the task was almost completed, Dr. Salkinson wrote:

My Hebrew version of the New Testament is now ready for publication. Hebrew translation seems to be the only talent given to me, and I have consecrated it unto the Lord. It is my alabaster box of precious ointment which I pour out in honor of my Savior, that the fragrance of His name may fill the whole house of Israel.

Unfortunately, Dr. Salkinson died before the work of translation was completely finished, and Dr. Ginsburg completed the work. For some time the translation was known as the Salkinson-Ginsburg New Testament, and it has been instrumental in communicating the knowledge of Christ to many thousands of Jews.

In Salkinson's last days, when he was afflicted with a painful and increasing loss of sight, a Jew said to him,

"Your suffering in the eyes is a due punishment for your work [nightly reading and writing] on the New Testament, with which you are going to dim the light of Israel." Salkinson replied, "If my present dimness has been caused by that work, I am comforted with the hope that that work will enlighten many an eye in Israel."

His service for the Master and his fellow Jews was of paramount importance, even to the point of self-effacement. We know that when his work on earth was done he received the Master's welcoming word: "Well done, thou good and faithful servant: . . . enter thou into the joy of thy Lord" (Matt. 25:21).

27

Author and Preacher
1831–1890

Aaron Adolph Saphir

IN THE EARLY nineteenth century the Jews of Hungary were insular and exclusive. They considered it sinful to engage in the study of any literature other than the sacred writings of Israel, particularly the Talmud and its commentaries. Contemporary science and secular literature were ignored. But there were exceptions—those in the general community who sought to revitalize and reform Jewish life and thought.

Among the reformers was Israel Saphir, who worked ceaselessly to encourage intellectual freedom and cultural development among his fellow Jews. To this end he founded a Jewish educational institution in Budapest for the children of socially advanced Jews. His home was open to progressive Jews of like mind. Into this environment, his son Aaron Adolph was born on September 18, 1831.

Adolph's mother also was both cultured and pious. She was a member of one of Hungary's leading and highly respected families, many of whose forebears had been distinguished for their learning. She was a woman of fine character and gentle nature. With parents of such qualities of character and intellect it was natural that Adolph inherited something of their tastes and talents. Indeed, he wrote of his father:

> My father was a good Hebrew scholar, and had intimate knowledge of German, French, and English literature. He also pursued with zeal philosophical and theological studies, and rendered much service to the cause of education in Hungary.

In his early boyhood, Adolph gave many indications that he would become a man of exceptional ability. At the age of four he attended the school which his father had founded. Such early attendance at the place of learning is reminiscent of Rabbi Joshua, of whom it is said in the Talmud that his mother carried him to school while he was yet an infant, so that his ear might become accustomed to the words of the teacher.

But the factor of supreme importance in Adolph's life is that he was led to Christ. The first step in the events leading to his conversion was, in fact, the conversion of his father. Adolph's uncle, M. G. Saphir, a noted humorous writer, had become a Christian. Israel Saphir, though at first shocked by the news, decided to inquire into the matter and discover, if possible, some justification for his brother's action. He procured all the books he could find dealing with the credibility of the Christian religion. At that time he had retired from business and was able to devote the greater part of his time to study. He therefore gave himself especially to the study of the New Testament and other Christian writings.

During these inquiries he met Dr. Duncan of the Scottish mission in Budapest, and under the pretext of seeking to improve his knowledge of English, regularly attended Dr. Duncan's services, accompanied by his son Adolph. Dr. Duncan's sermons made a deep impression upon both father and son, although Adolph was at that time only twelve years of age. Gradually the light dawned upon them, and they both came to Jesus to find rest and peace for their troubled hearts. Israel Saphir was convinced beyond any possible doubt that Jesus of Nazareth was indeed the one "of whom Moses in the law, and the prophets did write." Adolph found what his soul longed for, the presence of Jehovah—God in Christ.

Later in life, in one of his lectures, Dr. Adolph Saphir recalled his life before he became a Christian:

> Perhaps none of you know from experience what it is to live without the knowledge of the incarnation; what it is to endeavor

to realize the incomprehensible, infinite God, without the light and comfort of the Mediator, and how joyous and self-evidencing is the peaceful brightness when Jesus is revealed as the Son of God, declaring the Father.

I was brought up in my childhood in the synagogue, and was taught that there was one God, infinite, incomprehensible Holy Spirit; high above us and omnipresent. Much stress was laid on the unity and the unicity of God. But this bare, vague, and abstract monotheism leaves the mind in darkness, while the heart is chilly and desolate.

There was another and better current which then influenced me. It was the national history as recorded in the books of Moses, the Psalms, and the Prophets, and commemorated in the festivals. There I was met by no abstract idea of unicity, but by a loving God, who appeared unto Abraham and spoke to him, who led Israel through the wilderness and dwelt among them; and after, when I thought of the friendly, kind, concrete human way in which the Lord God then appeared unto His people and dwelt with them, I wondered why He was not now with us, known, loved, and followed.

One day I was looking at some books, and the title of one arrested my eye. It was *Die Menschenwerdung Gottes*—God Becoming Man. The thought went through my mind like a flash of lightning; it thrilled my soul with the most joyous solemnity. "Oh," I said, "this would be the most beautiful thing, if God were to become man and visit us!"

Not many years after, I heard about Jesus, and read the Gospels. I felt here the same presence, the same loving, condescending, redeeming, and sanctifying God, that appeared unto the fathers. I felt that here was Jehovah; that all darkness had disappeared, and that the grand but inconceivable glory here shone upon us in the perfect, peaceful, and holy countenance of the man Christ Jesus.

Peniel! "I have seen God face to face, and my life is preserved. . . ." To believe in Jesus, the Son of God, is not an abstract dogma or a theosophic speculation, but a soul experience, a new heart-life. It is the mystery of godliness.

In his preface to the *Memoirs of Adolph Saphir*, Rev. Gavin Carlyle touched upon this high degree of spirituality so manifest in Saphir's thought:

> The freshness and originality of his ideas and expressions, and above all his spiritual power, [gave Dr. Saphir] deep insight into the meaning of Scripture and the relations of the different parts. The expression "mighty in the Scriptures" truly describes him. In his commanding knowledge of the spirit and purport of the various books of the Bible, few preachers of his own or any age approach him. He foreshadows in this what great results may be anticipated from the promised restoration of Israel.

From age thirteen to seventeen, Saphir was educated at the Gymnasium in Berlin. He resided at the home of Rev. Charles Schwartz, the husband of his oldest sister. Here he became acquainted with the Rev. Theodore Meyer, a Hebrew Christian who was formerly a rabbi, and they became lifelong friends.

In all this, Saphir never forgot, or ceased to be grateful for, the influences which had transformed his life. The mission in Budapest which had proved such a blessing to him and the members of his family, had been established by Scottish missionaries to the Jews, and therefore Saphir's thoughts turned toward Scotland. He desired to pursue his studies there. After passing the necessary qualifying examinations, he was admitted to the second class of undergraduates at the University of Glasgow. There, and at Marischal College, Aberdeen, he took all the subjects prescribed for the study of theology. After obtaining good certificates, and taking the first prize for Greek in Aberdeen, he became a student of theology in the Free Church College in Edinburgh. In Glasgow he took the bachelor of arts degree.

After a brief period of service as missionary to the Jews in Hamburg, and later to Germans in Glasgow, Saphir was called to the work of the Christian ministry in England. He served for five years as minister of the Laygate Presbyterian Church in South Shields. From 1861 to 1872 he was minister of St. Mark's Presbyterian Church, Greenwich, and served with such conspicuous ability that the church had to be enlarged twice, and the congregation increased from one hundred worshipers to one thousand.

From Greenwich he moved to the charge of a church in Notting Hill, and the church there was soon filled to overflowing with believers eager to hear his expositions of Scripture. He established a Thursday morning series of lectures, the most outstanding of which were his remarkable lectures on the Epistle to the Hebrews and the divinity of our Lord. Carlyle refers to this period as "the great triumph of his career."

Unfortunately, Saphir's dedication to study and to the claims of the pastoral office affected his health, and in 1875 his health broke under the strain. He was so seriously weakened that frequently great exhaustion followed his occupation of the pulpit twice on Sunday. The strain was eased for a time through the help of assistants. But increasing physical weakness necessitated frequent absences from his work. This so preyed upon his sensitive nature that, sadly, he felt compelled to resign the charge.

After prolonged rest, and with a measure of renewed strength, Saphir responded in 1882 to a call addressed to him from the Belgrave Presbyterian Church. He ministered there until 1888. In that year his own uncertain health and the illness of his wife led him to retire from the permanent pastorate and to serve the churches as health and opportunity might allow. He preached his last sermon when he deputized for a sick pastor, just six weeks before his own death, and his text was: "Enoch walked with God and he was not for God took him." Mrs. Saphir died only a few days before him, and he passed to his reward in his sixtieth year.

Dr. Saphir was also a prolific and powerful writer. His works included: *Expository Lectures on the Epistle to the Hebrews; The Hidden Life; Our Life Day; The Life of Faith.* His biographer, Gavin Carlyle, refers appreciatively to his pulpit power:

> He seemed to combine the gentleness and simplicity of a child with the firm grasp of a strong man when he dealt with Holy Scripture. No halting or hesitating utterance could be detected in his voice or manner as he dwelt upon the deep things of God and lucidly spread out before a hushed audience the magnificent truths concerning Jesus Christ and God's way of salvation. There was none of the obscurity, which sometimes passes for profundity, in his preaching: very young listeners understood his meaning; experienced believers were enriched by his discourses; anxious souls were comforted; doubting ones found deliverance.
>
> Like his great countryman, St. Paul, whom he resembled in the weakness of his body, as well as in spiritual insight and might, he "shunned not to declare to his hearers the whole counsel of God," and his faithfulness found a reward even here in the large circle of attached and appreciative Christian friends from every evangelical branch of the Christian church. He rests from his labors, and his works do follow him.

28

Philologist and
Translator
1831–1895

Joseph
Schereschewsky

"AMONG THE MEN and women who consider it their blessed work to bring the Word of God within the reach of far-off tribes by means of translations in their native idioms we may single out Bishop Schereschewsky, the Christian Jew." This remarkable tribute was expressed, not by a Christian, but by a rabbi: Rabbi Dr. Max L. Margolis, in *The Story of Bible Translations.*

Joseph Schereschewsky was the son of poor, orthodox parents, and was born in Tauroggen, in Russian Lithuania, on May 6, 1831. It was the desire of his parents that he should become a rabbi, and with that purpose in view his father arranged for him to be educated at the Rabbinical Academy of Zhitomir. But rabbinical studies, and the Judaism in which he was instructed, held no appeal for Joseph. He therefore left the academy and entered the German university of Breslau to study oriental languages. There, a Hebrew New Testament came into his possession, and after a diligent and careful perusal of it he was convinced that Jesus of Nazareth was the Jewish Messiah.

Feeling that he could not openly confess Christ before his fellow Jews of Lithuania, he decided to emigrate to America. He was then twenty-three years of age. As he was traveling to the

United States via Hamburg, a Jewish missionary by the name of Jacobi, who lived and worked in the northern German city, supplied him with a letter of commendation to Pastor John Neander, a Jewish missionary in New York. When Schereschewsky arrived in New York the pastor received him most cordially, and introduced him as a gifted scholar of great promise to other Jewish missionaries, and to interested and well-disposed Christians.

A year later, Schereschewsky openly confessed his faith in Christ and was baptized, and shortly afterwards entered the Presbyterian Theological Seminary in Allegheny, Pennsylvania. He graduated in the spring of 1858, but owing to certain theological scruples he left the Presbyterian church and joined the Protestant Episcopal church. In the autumn of that year he graduated from the Episcopal Preachers' Seminary, and in 1859 was ordained deacon in St. George's Church in New York City.

Following his ordination he felt the divine call to preach the gospel to the people of China, and the Protestant Episcopal Mission Society appointed him to that country. Bishop Boone and other missionaries accompanied him to Shanghai, where he was first stationed. Within a year Bishop Boone recognized Schereschewsky's linguistic gifts and ordained him to the priesthood. The bishop then sent him to Peking for the special purpose of studying the main dialects of China, colloquial as well as literary. Schereschewsky's studies included Mandarin Chinese as well as High and Low Wenli. It then became his task to revise and complete the existing (and somewhat deficient) translation of the Bible. Schereschewsky also played a large part in the translation of the Episcopalian prayer book into Mandarin Chinese; this was published in 1865.

While on a visit to Shangai in 1868 he met Susannah Waring, a missionary teacher, and shortly afterwards they were married. She accompanied him back to Peking, where she taught in the mission school while he worked on the translation of the Bible into the Mandarin dialect. The translation was finished in 1875. In addition to this enormous and demanding task, Schereschewsky preached regularly to audiences who came from far and near to hear him. On completing his translation, he, his wife, and their two children went to America.

So valuable and effective was his work as translator and missionary that his church appointed him bishop of Shanghai.

Initially, being a very modest man, he declined to accept the honor, but when a year later the appointment was again pressed upon him, he gratefully accepted it. Thus, on October 1, 1877, he was solemnly consecrated mission bishop of Shanghai in Grace Church, New York, by the resident Bishop Smith in the presence of fourteen bishops and five other clergymen. Two American colleges conferred on him the title Doctor of Theology.

Schereschewsky remained in America for two years, during which time he secured financial help from many quarters for the establishing of a mission college in China. He returned to China in the spring of 1878, and on April 14, 1879, laid the cornerstone for St. John's College, a school for the instruction of national teachers and pastors. This was the first Protestant college in China.

Two years after the laying of the foundation stone, and in his fiftieth year, Schereschewsky was stricken by a serious illness which left him totally paralyzed. His physicians ordered him to Geneva, where he was under treatment from 1882 to 1886. He was unwilling to retain an office whose duties he could not fulfill, and so resigned his bishopric. When only partially recovered from his paralysis (he still could not speak), he and his family returned to America. Despite his disabilities, Schereschewsky continued to work on his translation of the Bible into the Wenli dialect. Although he was in constant pain and almost helpless through his paralysis, he persevered in training his index fingers to operate an English typewriter.

His enormous task of translation was finished in 1895, and shortly after its completion Schereschewsky, his wife, and their daughter returned to China. From then on he devoted his time to transferring the romanized text of his Bible into Chinese characters. He worked in Shanghai for almost two years, ably assisted by several Christian secretaries. Later he was commissioned by the American Bible Society and went to Tokyo, where he was to supervise the printing of a revised version of the Old Testament in the Mandarin dialect. The first version of his work was published in 1875 in Peking. After completing his work for the American Bible Society, Schereschewsky gave himself to the translation of the whole Bible in Wenli, and brought this effort to a satisfactory conclusion shortly before his death.

After the first publication of the Old Testament in Mandarin, in 1875, a special commission of the American Episcopal church reported:

> Dr. Schereschewsky translated from Hebrew into the Mandarin language—a language which is understood by people four times more than the number of people who live in the United States. This his work is one of the most marvelous achievements of the human spirit, one of the noblest triumphs of missionary zeal and missionary erudition.

A further tribute was written by the Rev. Theodosius S. Tyng:

> Judged by results, the most important thing [Schereschewsky did was] determination of mission policy in the Far East. Without Bishop Schereschewsky and his work as founder of St. John's College in Shanghai, I doubt if we should ever have had St. Paul's College in Tokyo, or Boone University in China. That now . . . we have those widely known institutions, with the great forces that have already come from them, is certainly due to him more than to any other man.

His translation of the Bible into colloquial and literary Chinese made it possible for 250,000,000 people to know the Word of God. His translation of the Episcopal Prayer was also of great value, and was widely used. He prepared a concordance in Chinese to the entire Bible, and worked on a translation of the Apocrypha which was unfinished at his death. He wrote grammars and dictionaries to help missionaries in the study of Chinese. His mastery of the language can be gauged from the statement of the great philologist Dr. Maxwell Miller: "Schereschewsky is one of the six most learned Orientalists in the world."

Truly the Lord is glorified in His servants, and in the way in which He led Schereschewsky to such heights of achievement in the promulgation of the good tidings. Innumerable men and women of the East owe their knowledge of Christ to him, and it is appropriate to quote the following extract from the Bible Society's memoir, written by the Rev. Craydon Edmund:

> His version of the Old Testament, first published by the American Bible Society in 1875, has since been repeatedly issued by both the American Bible Society and the British and Foreign Bible Society. A revised version appeared in 1899. But a still greater work was his translation of the whole Bible into easy

Wenli. He added the New Testament in this case in order to secure uniformity. (The former versions were in a somewhat different style.) This Bible the American Society published in 1902.

The significance of Bishop Schereschewsky's achievements, however, lies not so much in their extent and scholarship as in their testimony to the indomitable courage of the man and to his devotion to his work. . . .

As a translator his influence has been far wider than it could have been as a bishop, and Chinese Christians will ever remember, with gratitude to God, the great scholar who out of weakness was made strong—who laid so well and so truly the foundation of the Bible in [Chinese] vernacular and in the more popular form of their written language.

A further tribute, expressed by Rev. William Bacon Stevens in *The Protestant Episcopal Church and the Bible,* records:

The grandest conquests of the world's mightiest heroes sink into littleness beside the work [of] Bishop Schereschewsky . . . when he made the Bible speak in Mandarin and heralded out salvation over half a hemisphere.

29

Charles Andrew Schonberger

CHARLES ANDREW SCHONBERGER was born into an orthodox Jewish family in the Hungarian town of Mor in 1841. He was one of ten children, and grew up in a happy home and closely-knit family life. His elementary education was at the local school, but he was sent to Budapest to continue his studies.

One day, he visited a fellow student whose father was ill. The sick man asked Schonberger to read aloud to him from a particular book. The book was the New Testament, and the portion selected was the Sermon on the Mount. Charles, who was then 18 years of age, had never seen—or even heard of—the New Testament, and its message claimed his absorbed attention.

When he again visited his friend he was introduced to Mr. Israel Saphir, Dr. Adolph Saphir's father (see chap. 27). Mr. Saphir lived in the same house and took a warm interest in the young inquirer. He invited Charles to his apartment and presented him with a copy of the New Testament. Schonberger studied the volume diligently and, following special instruction by Mr. Saphir and others, confessed his faith in Christ. On

May 5, 1864, he was baptized in the Hungarian Reformed church.

After he became a Christian, Schonberger found himself, like many other Jewish believers, rejected and spurned by his family and Jewish friends. He had to endure severe trials and much persecution. He gained many new friends, however, including the entire Saphir family. In 1871 he married Mr. Saphir's youngest daughter. Dr. Adolph Saphir, who at that time was the minister of a church in London, came to his assistance, and made it possible for him to study at the English Presbyterian College in London. Later he studied under the renowned Professor Franz Delitzsch of the universities of Erlangen and Leipzig.

On completing his studies in 1868, Schonberger held two assistantships in Budapest and Prague, both in connection with the Free Church of Scotland Mission. In 1872 he accepted appointment as missionary in Prague of the British Society for the Propagation of the Gospel Among the Jews. After he was ordained in 1874, Schonberger frequently occupied the pulpits of evangelical churches, and was repeatedly invited to take settled pastorates. He preferred, however, to give his life to work among the Jews. In pursuit of this objective he set himself to win the interest and attention of educated Jews by means of public lectures. These attracted large and attentive audiences.

Eleven years after his appointment as missionary in Prague he was transferred to Vienna, where he succeeded the gifted missionary, Dr. Isaac Salkinson (see chap. 26), translator of the New Testament into Hebrew. In Vienna he found unlimited opportunities for witness, and was able to make contact with many Jews from all parts of Austria. To his great sorrow he found that anti-Semitism was both widespread and aggressive, and he spent much time and effort in combatting it. Among the many Jews (mostly of the socially and culturally higher classes) whom he baptized during his eight years in Vienna were two of his own brothers.

Schonberger took a prominent part in the Rabinovich Movement in Russia (see Joseph Rabinowitz, chap. 24), and assisted Rabbi Lichtenstein (chap. 19) in Hungary. In 1887 he met David Baron (chap. 2) and they became lifelong friends. About seven years after their meeting they jointly founded the Hebrew Christian Testimony to Israel, a mission with which Schonberger was actively connected until his death in 1924.

In 1921, Schonberger settled in Berlin. He was eighty years old and nearly blind, a great handicap which made it difficult for him to travel from his home to the mission headquarters in London. But the mission had large quarters in Berlin, so Schonberger took an apartment on the premises. There was a good-sized meeting room and Schonberger made full use of the opportunities presented to him of preaching to the many Jews who attended the meetings. He preferred to live on the premises so that, in his own words, he "might die in harness."

Unfortunately, his life in Berlin was clouded by a great sorrow through the death of his only child, a gifted daughter. Other adverse factors weighed heavily upon him, but he remained firmly convinced that these were part of God's plan for him, and for the good of Israel. He died on July 8, 1924, at the age of 83, and his widow had his principle motto engraved on his tombstone: "Christ and Israel, and Israel and Christ are inseparable" (I Cor. 13:13).

Many tributes were paid to his Christian integrity, and to his work. A missionary colleague, Mr. J. L. Landsmann, testified:

From his very conversion onwards his express desire was to preach the gospel to his Jewish brethren. With this purpose in view he studied and prepared himself most thoroughly, for he wished to become an effective worker in the Jewish missionfield. To this early ideal he has remained true to [his death].

Although endowed by nature with great oratorical gifts that would have enabled him to fill any pulpit in the church with honor, he chose the obscurity of a Jewish missionary in order to minister to those who were in greatest need of his ministry. Here in England he has aspired to no worldly fame or honor, being satisfied [to] work ... among the poorer classes of his own people.

His friend and associate, David Baron, praised Schonberger's character and witness:

He was a man of comprehensive culture and thorough theological training, possessing a strongly independent mind, a forceful personality, and spiritual passion. His work was both attractive in form and weighty in substance. A sonorous voice and rich gifts of natural oratory combined with a varied knowledge of life and an experiential insight into the gospel, to make him an arresting and powerful preacher. A close student of the Scriptures, he specially brooded over the Prophets, which he made to speak to the Jewish soul in the language of today. He himself had not a little of the prophet's fire and intensity, and of his firm, uncompromising temper.

30

Writer and Lecturer
1802–1861

Friedrich Julius Stahl

IN THE NINETEENTH CENTURY many Jews of intellectual brilliance, cultural attainments, spiritual insight, and personal courage responded to the gospel. Friedrich Julius Stahl was an outstanding example. He was born in Munich on January 16, 1802, into a family of good social standing, public influence, and professional authority. Religiously the household was strictly orthodox, and Friedrich was educated in that tradition. His father was a banker, jurist, and publicist.

Bavarian Jews were at that time subject to various restrictions, and it was an event of some significance when young Stahl was accepted as a student at the local Gymnasium. He was, in fact, the first Jewish boy to be so admitted. Through his studies, observations, and the general associations of the school, a completely new world was revealed to him. During his time at the Gymnasium, Stahl gained a view of the truths and ideals of the Christian faith completely different from the view taught in his Jewish environment. His new perception was further confirmed through his studies at the Institute of Philosophy under the pious Friedrich Thiersch. As a result, when Stahl was 17 years old he was fully convinced that Jesus of Nazareth was his Redeemer, Israel's Messiah, and the Savior of mankind. Stahl was baptized as an outward testimony of his decision.

As was to be expected, his father was greatly shocked when he heard of his son's conversion and resolved to disown and disinherit him. He soon learned, however, that his son's conversion was the result of deep personal conviction and brought him great happiness, and he quietly accepted the situation. Later he forgave Friedrich and closely observed his manner of life as a Christian. Friedrich's testimony in behavior and conversation so impressed his father, mother, and seven of his brothers and sisters that they too became convinced and consistent believers.

After his conversion and baptism, Friedrich's first intention was to study theology, but he later decided that he could best serve his Master by studying law. This he did at the universities of Wurzburg, Erlangen, and Heidelberg. In his twenty-fifth year he gained the degree of Doctor of Law. The following year he became lecturer at the University of Munich, and published his first book on Roman law. This was followed by several other books which aroused great attention. He was later appointed professor at Erlangen.

At that time he became involved in the struggle for the rights and freedom of the evangelical church in Bavaria, which labored under numerous restrictions imposed by the Jesuitical enactments of the Bavarian government. As champion of the Protestant cause Stahl was elected to Parliament, where he fearlessly worked for the rights of Protestantism. For this he suffered government persecution, but he also received encouragement from many parts of Germany. In fact, the crown prince of Prussia, on ascending the throne as Friedrich Wilhelm IV, invited Dr. Stahl to Berlin to serve in the university as professor of law and philosophy. In Berlin he gained great fame as a participant in several national movements. His lectures were attended not only by students, but also by many persons of exalted rank in public life.

As political movements gathered momentum and, in 1848, as revolution threatened to overthrow both throne and altar, Dr. Stahl stepped forward as the outspoken defender of the royal and priestly prerogatives. As a result of his unfaltering activities in defense of church and state, he became the head of the Conservative Party in Prussia. He also held the highest position in the state's government of the church, and was referred to as "the beloved unopposed head of confessional Lutheranism in the realm of ecclesiastical affairs."

In addition to his uncompromising stand for legal, fiscal, and ecclesiastical principles, he also stood firm on doctrinal matters. He opposed vigorously the errors of Hegelian philosophy. In his book *Philosophy des Rechts* he sought to show that philosophy is not the ultimate objective of God, but that God must be the ultimate objective of philosophy. He called science to "repentance," which caused a great furor among jurists and philosophers. Stahl viewed Christianity as a renovating force that would eventually renew the dead world and save it from a decaying morality:

> Christianity is the fountain of life, which springing up in inexhaustible fullness, furnishes a force by which the downfallen are raised up, the weak strengthened, the sinner sanctified. And the vision of self-sacrifice, which has glimmered through the poetry of the ages, shines out in its fullness, in Christ, who gave Himself for the sin of the world.

Stahl based his view of law and political science on Christian revelation, denied rationalistic doctrines and, as a deduction from this premise, maintained that a state church must be strictly confessional. Of this the renowned jurist and steadfast Christian Rev. J. F. de le Roi spoke in his book, *Friedrich Julius Stahl*:

> Friedrich Stahl, the evangelical Christian of Israel, stands out as a great reminder of the principle that Christianity, especially the evangelical faith, must pervade the life and actions of the state, society, the church, and science. . . .

And in an article in the *Realencyclopedie fur Protestantische Theologie und Kirche* (vol. viii, p. 75), de le Roi summed up Stahl's life and labor:

> To young men of science Stahl was an inspiring leader and counselor. Though living on a meager professorial salary, he filled three important positions of church and state without remuneration. So stands the picture of Stahl in the memory of the German evangelical church as that of a noble son of Israel.

Dr. Friedrich Stahl died when he was only 59 years of age, on August 10, 1861. He was buried in St. Matthew's cemetery in Berlin.

31

Henry Aaron Stern

"THE GREATEST man among Hebrew Christians . . . a mighty influence in bringing Jews to Christ was Henry Aaron Stern." So wrote the Rev. Isaac Levinsohn, chief secretary of the British Society for the Propagation of the Gospel Among the Jews from 1899 to 1919.

Henry Aaron Stern was born on April 11, 1820, in a small town in the duchy of Hesse-Cassel. A few years later the family moved to Frankfurt-am-Main, and Henry spent his early years in the "Judengasse," the Jewish quarter of Frankfurt. His education was planned with a view to his becoming a doctor of medicine. But Henry himself was very ambitious, and he went to Hamburg where, in his judgment, there were greater opportunities for young men pursuing a commercial career.

But God had His own plan for the young man. One day, while he was walking along one of the streets of Hamburg, Stern noticed some Hebrew and German books displayed in a glass case. Pausing to see what was written in the open pages he discovered that the case and its contents belonged to a missionary who sought to win Jews to faith in Christ. Like most other Jews, however, Stern harbored deep feelings of resentment toward missionaries, the claims they made, and the teachings they propagated. But the Scriptures displayed, and their references to Christ, made a strong impression upon him. He tried hard to eradicate the impression from his mind, but without success; it was too strong and insistent. The seed of the Word had fallen on fallow ground.

When Stern was only 19 years old he journeyed to London, where he hoped to find security, satisfaction, and prosperity. But he was quickly disillusioned. Instead of finding wealth and satisfaction on the world scene he found frustration. The worldly hopes he set his heart upon turned ashes. But God was working all things together for his good.

A young fellow-lodger invited him to attend a meeting to hear what the missionaries—the "apostates"—had to say. Out of curiosity, and remembering what he had seen in the showcase in Hamburg, he went to the meeting in the Palestine Place Chapel of the London Society for Promoting Christianity Among the Jews. The meeting was conducted by Dr. Caul, a prominent missionary to the Jews. Stern was so impressed by what he saw and heard that he attended the meetings frequently. Ultimately in 1840, he was led to accept Christ as his Savior.

Stern abandoned his secular business interests and went to live in the "Operative Jewish Converts' Institution." In due course, having shown a special aptitude for missionary work, he was admitted as a student to the missionary college. In January, 1884, in his twenty-fourth year, Stern was accepted as a candidate for holy orders, and was appointed to initiate a mission to the Jews of Chaldea and Persia. He undertook the work in association with Mr. and Mrs. Murray Vickers, and with them proceeded to Jerusalem. Soon after their arrival, Stern and Vickers were ordained to the ministry, and on July 14, 1844, they received deacon's orders from the Jewish-Christian bishop of Jerusalem. The following September they began their missionary labors in Baghdad among a population of 16,000 Jews.

The message and the ministry of Stern aroused keen interest among the Jews. In fact, the number of inquirers became so great that the Jewish leaders became alarmed, and threatened to excommunicate any Jew who visited the missionaries. As a result, for some months no Jew dared be seen in their company. During this frustrating time, Stern occupied himself with missionary journeys into Persia, where he distributed the Scriptures and preached to large groups of eager inquirers, some of whom subsequently confessed their faith in baptism.

When the effect of the Jewish ban began to diminish Stern resumed his work in Baghdad. For a while there was no open antagonism, but the baptism of a Jewish doctor provoked a resurgence of the opposition. After this instance, however, the Jews were not intimidated by the threat of excommunication. Many frequented the mission and some were baptized.

After six years of witness in Baghdad and in itinerant missionary activity throughout Persia, Stern returned to England, and was ordained priest by the bishop of London. In April, 1850 he married Charlotte Elizabeth Purday, and the following June returned with his wife to Baghdad. During the next seven years he traveled with the gospel to the Jews of Persia, Constantinople, and Arabia, and to the Karaite Jews (see p. 79) in the Crimea. In Arabia, mostly among Yemeni Jews, his preaching in native costume brought multitudes to the synagogue to hear him. Following this period he again visited England, where he aroused intense interest in his work of evangelizing Jews in far-off lands. Then he returned to Constantinople to find new work awaiting him.

At that time attention was being drawn to the Jews of Abyssinia, the *Falashas* or exiles. These dark-skinned Jews claimed to be the descendants of adventurous Jews who, following the queen of Sheba's visit to Solomon, sought their fortune in her country. Of them Stern wrote:

> They claim lineal descent from Abraham, Isaac, and Jacob, and pride themselves on the fame of their progenitors and the purity of the blood that circulates in their own veins. The Law of Moses, which they profess to observe, is the formula after which they have molded their worship, and it sounds strange to hear in central Africa of a Jewish altar and atoning sacrifices. They observe the Jewish feasts, Passover, Pentecost and [the Feast of] Tabernacles. They also keep the Day of Atonement.

They were not familiar with the Jewish post-biblical writings, however, and thus did not know of the feasts of Purim and Hanukah. They knew nothing of the Talmud.

So far as the Christian faith was concerned the Falashas saw only the idolatrous and corrupt form of Christianity practiced by the Abyssinian church. In view of the need and the opportunity, Stern was urged to undertake a mission to the Falashas.

He accepted the task, trusting in the strength of the Lord of Hosts.

Before beginning his ministry, Stern had to obtain the sanction of King Theodorus, the ruler of Abyssinia, and the approval of the archbishop and metropolitan of the Abyssinian church. After obtaining their permission he visited the Falasha districts and was welcomed by the people, who desired to receive copies of the Bible, and were willing to hear the missionary's message. The contrast between the vain and superstitious idolatry they saw in the national church, and the simplicity of the record which God had given in His Word concerning His son, attracted them.

At the request of the London Jews' Society, Dr. Stern returned to England in 1861 to report on the success of this extraordinary mission, and to gather new support. After a two-year period in which he addressed large gatherings in various parts of the United Kingdom, he returned to Abyssinia. His joy knew no bounds when he found many converts awaiting his arrival and ready to cooperate with him in his work.

Greatly to his sorrow, however, Stern discovered that the king had become hostile toward mission work. One of the causes of the king's change of heart was the slight he imagined he had received from the British government by their ignoring his request to send an embassy to the Queen of England. Therefore, when Stern presented himself before the king to pay his respects, he found him full of indignation and inflamed by alcohol.

"Knock him down! Brain him! Kill him!" cried the enraged monarch.

"In the twinkling of an eye," wrote Stern, "I was stripped and on the ground insensible; stunned, unconscious and almost lifeless, with blood oozing out of scores of gashes, and I was dragged into the camp...."

For three and a half years Stern was kept in captivity, and subjected to physical and mental torture, in company with other victims of the monarch's rage. Release came only when the tyrant was overthrown as a result of a British military expedition.

Dr. Stern's letters, written during the long days of his captivity in Abyssinia reveal his spirit of dedication to the cause of the gospel:

Thank God, in the midst of my troubles, cares and anxieties, I enjoy the profoundest calm and resignation. It is true there are days when the heart pulsates with gratitude and joy, and there are days when it throbs beneath the mortifying agonies of despondency. Sometimes I feel as if I could not endure another week the fetters which encircle my limbs, and confine me in painful inactivity to this desolate rock. Such rebellious sentiments I generally try to suppress, and if this is impossible, I seek comfort in the thought, that all is ordered in wisdom and infinite love. Our heavenly Father hath, no doubt, an object in this protracted captivity and when once the veil of mystery is lifted up, every incident and circumstance which hath wrung a prayer or extorted a groan from the grieved soul, will prove to have been in harmony with the designs of a gracious Providence, and fraught with inestimable blessings. . . .

The Bible, prayers, and a morning and evening exposition of an appropriate passage were the exercises in which we regularly engaged. No bitter gibes, no harsh expressions, no unbecoming word characterised our intercourse. . . . When I looked on the devout countenances that there hung over the inspired page, as I commented on the selected text, I cherished the pleasing hope that the clouds, so big with wrath, had been charged with showers of everlasting mercy. At such a period—I say it solemnly—the punctured head, the riven side, the pierced feet, and the heavy cross of redeeming love, is a sight that nerves and supports the drooping and despondent spirit. In my distress and sorrow, I threw myself on the bosom of a sympathizing Savior. . . .

Stern and his fellow missionaries returned to England in June, 1868. For some time after his return Dr. Stern narrated his experiences to crowded audiences in every part of the country. He was heard with intense interest as he told the harrowing story of the Abyssinian mission. In 1871 he succeeded Dr. Ewald as head of the London mission of the London Society for Promoting Christianity Among the Jews. Ten years later the Archbishop of Canterbury conferred upon him the degree of Doctor of Divinity.

The last fifteen years of Stern's life were devoted to "the King's business" among the Jews of England. He gave special sermons, visited homes, and distributed tracts. His sermons were heard by large numbers who were attracted by his prominence as a preacher, and by his eloquence as he pointed his listeners to Jeshuah-haMashiach—Jesus the Messiah.

Dr. Stern's missionary activities were carried on from a mission hall situated in Whitechapel, the Jewish quarter in the East End of London. Regular meetings were held on Saturdays, and on some weekdays, with attendance often between four and five hundred Jews. There was also a daily Bible class for Jews, and numerous conversions and baptisms. Dr. Stern held special services for Jews in many other towns, and served as superviser of the "Wanderers' Home," an institution for the reception of inquirers and converts. Dr. Stern himself declared that in eight years he had baptized 134 Jews, excluding children.

Beside being an eloquent preacher and competent missionary, Dr. Stern was an accomplished writer. His published works dealing with his missionary work in the East included: *Dawning of Light in the East* (1854), an account of his work in Persia, Kurdistan, and Mesopotamia; *Wanderings Among the Falashas in Abyssinia;* and *The Captive Missionary.* His zeal and versatility made him an outstanding missionary. As one of his biographers wrote:

> No one can estimate the abundance of spiritual harvest from the long life of toil and labor which Stern spent to the honor and glory of his Master. He sowed in tears. He led captivity captive. He turned many to righteousness. And of him it may confidently be said that he will shine as a star for ever and ever.

Dr. Henry Aaron Stern's journeys to distant tribes, his endurance of suffering for Christ's sake, and his ceaseless labors for his Master, came to an end on May 13, 1885, when he passed into the presence of the Lord to find peace at the last before Him who is the "Prince of Peace." He was buried in the City of London Cemetery at Ilford.

32

*Rabbi, Evangelist,
and Bible Expositor*

Max Wertheimer

MAX WERTHEIMER was born in the province of Baden in Germany, and his devoutly religious father hoped that as a steadfast Jew his son would grow up to be a credit and an honor to his family. To this end he provided Max with a strictly Jewish education. From the age of five he was required to study the Pentateuch in Hebrew together with Rashi's commentary,[1] as well as parts of the Talmud. To ensure that his education was truly comprehensive he also attended the village school. At the age of eleven he gained admission to the Gymnasium at Ettenheim, where he studied for five years. Throughout his years at school he attended the synagogue regularly, and participated in its services. At home he observed the laws and customs, and said the various prayers required of the observant Jew.

In accordance with his parents' wishes, Wertheimer prepared himself for a commercial career. When he had gained sufficient knowledge and experience, he was engaged by a well-known manufacturing house in Strassburg, Alsace. In that beautiful

1. The commentaries of Rashi (Rabbi Shelomo ben Yitzhak, 1040–1105) are the basis of the traditional study of the Hebrew Bible and the Talmud.

city he spent the greater part of his spare time in reading and study and, as he himself acknowledges, in the enjoyment of worldly pleasures and indulgences.

But his worldliness robbed him of his peace of mind. He yearned for something nobler and more enduring, something that would give meaning to his life. In his youthful search for satisfaction and fulfillment he emigrated to the United States. For a while he lived in Buffalo, New York, where he attended the Franklin Street public school. Shortly after his arrival in Buffalo he met the rabbi of the Jewish temple. Through his instrumentality Wertheimer was helped by the temple congregation to enter the Hebrew Union College at Cincinnati, Ohio, in the fall of 1882.

While studying at the Hebrew Union College he was granted a stipend by the board of governors. This was in response to the recommendation of the president of the college, Dr. Isaac M. Wise, leader of the Jewish Reform movement in America. After Wertheimer had matriculated, he was placed in the second-year class, and was thus able to complete in seven years the usual eight years' course. Dr. Wertheimer writes of that period:

My religious views were fostered by tradition, pride, and prejudice. I thought Judaism was the greatest religion and the most rational. I catered to the evolutionary theory and had some modernistic notions of free thought, held some socialistic doctrines, and thought that Moses was the greatest of the prophets and benefactors, and that no one excelled him in originality, genius and perfection. I had a mania for theater-going and loved the melodramatic performances, as well as symphony concerts and classic operas. I was fond of reading fiction, romances, detective stories, and current literature. I played the violin and practiced whenever I had a chance. Thus I was swayed by all that is implied in "the lust of the flesh, the lust of the eye, and the pride of life. . . ."

In the Hebrew Union College I was in a class of nine students. We studied the T'nach [the thirty-nine books of the Old Testament]; also Hebrew grammar and composition; as well as many sections of the Mishnah and a number of treatises covering many folio pages of the Gemara, mostly from the Babylonian Talmud; the works of Rambam or Moses Maimonides, his *Moreh Nebuchin (Guide of the Perplexed)* and his *Mishnah Torah;* the work of the Kusari; also Joseph Albo's writings; the Sulchan Aruch (ritual code); and Dr. Graetz's *History of the Jews.* Then homiletics, or the science of preaching; and hermeneutics, or the science of interpretation according to rabbinical principles; the laws of Jewish jurisprudence concerning mar-

riage and divorce; also the philosophical and analytical intro-
ductions into the various parts of the Talmud.

The president of the college favored Wertheimer in various
ways, and chose him as the tutor of the children of his second
wife. He also arranged for him to live with him in his country
home. Wertheimer graduated from Cincinnati University in
1887 and from the rabbinical seminary in 1889.

Following his graduation and period as tutor Wertheimer
received his first call to officiate as rabbi. This was given by the
B'nai Yeshurum Temple in Dayton, Ohio. He maintained the
post for ten years and was held in the highest esteem, receiving
many expressions of love and regard from his congregation. In
his Friday evening lectures he spoke with authority on subjects
of current interest—social, industrial, and economic questions,
monotheism, ethical culture, and the moral systems of the Jews.
In his Sabbath morning addresses his subjects were the weekly
sections of the Pentateuch followed by a corresponding section
of the prophets. On Sunday he taught Sunday school from eight
in the morning until five in the evening, with one hour inter-
mission for dinner. He prepared boys and girls for confirmation
by drilling them in the cardinal truths of Judaism. Great crowds
came to hear and to witness the confirmation exercises in the
temple on Shavuoth (the Feast of Weeks).

Such was Wertheimer's reputation as lecturer, teacher, and
preacher that he was frequently called upon to speak in literary
societies and in schools. He was even made an honorary
member of the Dayton Protestant Ministerial Association,
though its members and officers knew him as the rabbi of the
temple congregation. As a distinguished rabbi he also addressed Christian gatherings of various denominations, including some Roman Catholic institutions. In short, he was loved
and esteemed not only by Jews, but also by Christians. The
Jewish congregation was justly proud of its rabbi who had
gained such recognition and appreciation among non-Jews. As
a good "mixer," which a Reform rabbi is expected to be, he
became a member of a Masonic lodge and later a Chaplain of
the Mystic lodge. He also became a member of the B'nai B'rith.

At this time he married Hannah Affelder, a refined and cultured Jewish woman who was also a skilled pianist and organist. Their marriage was blessed with the birth of a hand-
some baby boy. But, three and a half years later when the

couple had a baby girl, Mrs.Wertheimer contracted childbirth fever. She died at the age of 23, after three months of suffering. The little girl was taken by her grandmother while Wertheimer himself cared for the boy.

The death of his beloved wife was a devasting blow to Max, and he became a broken, unhappy man. One day, as he was walking aimlessly through the streets, a stranger spoke to him and, placing his hand on Max's shoulder, remarked, "Rabbi, I am sorry for the domestic affliction that has befallen you. I think I can brace you up and ease your grief, if you don't mind coming to my house. Will you come?" The stranger was a local judge. Wertheimer accepted the invitation, and that evening went to the judge's home. He was then taken to a spiritualistic seance. During the journey to the medium's home the judge related how he, too, was heartbroken when his baby girl died, and how he was comforted after a friend took him to a spiritualistic seance.

On that occasion, and on several evenings afterwards, Dr. Wertheimer was greatly disturbed by extraordinary phenomena. There were mysterious tappings at night, and the sound of footsteps like those of his wife. These manifestations upset him so much that it became difficult for him to concentrate on composing his weekly lectures and sermons. This disruption of his accustomed habit and routine greatly interfered with his work.

As his ten-year period of rabbinical administration drew to a close, Wertheimer decided not to ask for reelection. He wrote:

Reform Judaism had no comfort for my trouble. I determined to resign my office and administration and step down and out, leaving the rabbinate. For two years of my domestic sorrow I had tried to get some tangible comfort out of the Talmud, Mishnah, and rabbinical doctrines, but found none that satisfied my soul's hunger and longings. I began to study, to search for more light. I was lonesome, harassed, and full of doubts. Thus ended my ten years' rabbinate! I was crushed and disappointed. My congregation was exceedingly kind to me and most considerate but, alas, in spiritual things there was coming to be a barrier between us. Here endeth another chapter! Was God providentially preparing me for something better?

Bereft of any real spiritual comfort, I became even more conscious of the void in my heart occasioned by the unexpected death of my young wife. Imperceptibly I was drawn into a study of the things of the hereafter. I asked myself, "Where is she who was the joy and companion of my few years of married life?

What has become of her talent for music? Where has that music gone? Where is the touch of the vanished hand and the sound of the voice that is still?"

While in this disturbed and confused state of mind Dr. Wertheimer came into contact with Mary Baker Eddy, the founder of Christian Science. After completing a prescribed course of study, paid for by Mrs. Eddy, he became a teacher of Christian Science in Dayton, Ohio, where he had previously officiated as rabbi. Within a very short time he was chosen as the First Reader of the First Church of Christ Scientist, Dayton.

In that environment he met a woman named Ruby Jewel, whom he married five years after the death of his first wife. But his search for peace, his hunger for light, and his quest for truth remained unsatisfied. His faith in Christian Science, which at first appealed to him, began to waver. Whereas he had thought it to be the ideal expression and development of true Judaism, he began to recognize the many discrepancies between it and the Judaism he knew and loved. Doubts began to annoy and to perplex him. He was especially concerned that Christian Science emphatically denied the essentiality of blood in religion, while Judaism as taught in the Old Testament was closely identified with the blood of sacrifices.

For long periods Wertheimer locked himself in his library studying, meditating, and supplicating God for light. As he searched the Scriptures his thoughts were repeatedly directed to Isaiah 53. Again and again his attention focused on the central figure of the chapter—"the righteous servant." He knew the rabbinical interpretation of the title "righteous servant," which was said to refer to the people of Israel, because they were required to bear the iniquities of the Gentiles. But as he read and pondered the passage he saw clearly that the prophet could not be referring to the people of Israel, since in his first chapter he speaks of Israel as the most sinful nation on earth.

Other rabbinical suggestions about the righteous servant intruded themselves into his thought, but none were in harmony with the fifty-third chapter of Isaiah. In meditation his thoughts were directed to a variety of Scripture passages. He considered "the Son of man" in Daniel 7:13-14:

I saw in the night visions, and, behold, one like the Son of man came with the clouds of heaven, and came to the Ancient of days, and they brought him near before him. And there was given him dominion, and glory, and a kingdom, that all people, nations, and languages, should serve him: his dominion is an everlasting dominion, which shall not pass away, and his kingdom that which shall not be destroyed.

He also studied the phrase, "The Lord said unto my Lord" in Psalm 110:1, as well as the "man" in heaven spoken of in the first chapter of Ezekiel. In addition his attention was drawn to Isaiah 9:6-7:

For unto us a child is born, unto us a son is given: and the government shall be upon his shoulder: and his name shall be called Wonderful, Counsellor, The Mighty God, The Everlasting Father, The Prince of Peace. Of the increase of his government and peace there shall be no end, upon the throne of David, and upon his kingdom, to order it, and to establish it with judgment and with justice from henceforth even for ever. The zeal of the Lord of hosts will perform this.

Gradually, these Old Testament passages, and many others, turned his thought to "the son of man [who] came not to be ministered unto, but to minister, and to give his life a ransom for many" (Mark 10:45)—the man of Calvary. Previously he had casually read parts of the New Testament, but had never felt any deep interest in its contents, except as a means to demonstrate his erudition at meetings with Christian clergymen. Now, however, he began to study it carefully and prayerfully. And the more he studied it the more he saw it to be complementary to the Old Testament. Christian doctrine which he had ridiculed as illogical, unnatural, and un-Jewish he now saw as perfectly logical and truly Jewish, although supernatural. He now found that such fundamental articles of faith as belief in the triune God, the divinity of Christ, and the virgin birth, were based solidly on the anticipations of the Old Testament. Dr. Wertheimer writes of the great moment when he reached the conviction that Jesus was Israel's Messiah and the Son of God:

I fell down on my knees and exclaimed, "Oh, Thou Jehovah Ye-s-ou-s art the only Savior, who didst make an atonement for my sins. It was Thou, Jehovah the Holy One of Israel, who was wounded for my transgressions and bruised for my iniquities, and the chastisement of my peace was upon Thee, and by Thy stripes I am healed. Give me faith to believe on Thee and to own Thee as my Savior, Messiah and Lord. Give me courage to confess Thee before men." Thus I passed from the shackles of rabbinical Judaism and the meshes of Christian Science into the government and Lordship of *Jeshua haMasshiach, ben Elohim, ben David*—of Jesus the Messiah, the Son of God, and the Son of David.

On March 30, 1904, Dr. Wertheimer publicly confessed Christ in the Central Baptist Church in Dayton, Ohio. He then entered the Southern Baptist seminary in Louisville, Kentucky, and graduated after one year of study. After his ordination he served as pastor for five years at Ada, Ohio, followed by two and a half years as pastor-evangelist with the New Covenant Mission in Pittsburg, Pennsylvania. Finally he felt called to a wider sphere as a "free-lance" preacher of the gospel to both Jew and Gentile. The greater part of his support in this ministry was provided by the income from his books. He was continually in great demand as Bible teacher, expositor, and evangelist.

33

Missionary, Traveler,
and Explorer
1795–1862

Joseph Wolff

JOSEPH WOLFF, who was born in Weilersbach, a small Bavarian village, in 1795, was one of the most outstanding missionaries of the nineteenth century. His father, David Wolff, was of the tribe of Levi, and was the rabbi of the small community numbering about fifteen families. Soon after Joseph's birth, however, the family moved to Halle.

Joseph received a strictly Jewish education, and at the age of six was able to recite the daily prayers in Hebrew. But when he was eleven years of age he was placed in the Protestant lyceum in Stuttgart. Growing dissatisfied with the school he went to live with his cousin Moses Cohen at Bamberg, where he entered the Roman Catholic lyceum. Impressed by its strong religious influence, he resolved to become a Christian and to be a missionary like Francis Xavier.[1]

Wolff was still unsettled and unsatisfied in his search for truth, however, and he traveled to various cities in Germany and Austria. Finally, in 1812, he reached Prague, where he was baptized at the age of 17 by the abbot of the Benedictine

---

1. Saint Francis Xavier (1506–52) was a Basque Jesuit missionary, called "the Apostle to the Indies."

monastery Emmaus. By this time he was proficient in the Latin, Persian, Chaldean, and Syriac languages. Returning to Austria, he entered the University of Vienna to study Arabic, ecclesiastical history, and theology. He remained there for two years.

To continue his studies in Oriental languages and theology, Wolff entered the Lutheran university at Tübingen in 1815, but left the following year on a pilgrimage to Rome, traveling on foot through Switzerland and Italy. In Rome he was introduced to Pope Pius VII, and entered the Collegio Romano. Because of his Protestant leanings, however, he was expelled within a year. He returned to Vienna in 1818. In his restlessness and uncertainty he entered one monastery after another until his disquietude brought him to Paris.

In Paris he made the acquaintance of Robert Haldane, who exercised a powerful religious influence over him. He accompanied Haldane to London in 1819. In England he came under the notice of well-known friends of Israel, including Mr. Henry Drummond, the Rev. Lewis Way, and the Rev. Charles Simeon. For a time he resided at Palestine Place, the missionary headquarters of the London Society for Promoting Christianity Among the Jews. While there he attended the services in the Episcopalian Jews' chapel and, as he himself expressed it, was "enchanted with the devotion and beauty of the ritual." From that time he considered himself to be a member of the Church of England.

The London society sent him to Cambridge for training as a missionary, to study theology under the Rev. Charles Simeon, and to study additional Oriental languages under Professor Lee. Such was Wolff's zeal and eagerness for active missionary service that two years' residence at Cambridge and a short course at the London society's seminary in Sussex were sufficient. At this point, therefore, Mr. Drummond (at his own expense) sent him forth with letters of introduction from the London society on his lifelong and fruitful mission. He left England on April 17, 1821. Traveling via Gibraltar and Malta he reached Egypt, where he spent three months among the Jews, preaching in their synagogues and distributing New Testaments.

During his journey he visited the monastery on Mount Sinai. Then he spent four months at Jerusalem preaching the gospel and circulating the Holy Scriptures among the various Jewish sects. Dr. Naudi, the church missionary society's correspondent in Malta, reported on the results of Wolff's two visits to Jerusalem:

> Jerusalem, until lately, was thought to be an impracticable place for missionary undertakings, and the Jews, inhabitants of Palestine, were considered an inaccessible people. . . . Mr. Wolff, I may venture to say, has cleared the way to these modern Jews, and himself succeeded in great measure with them.

The Rev. W. B. Lewis of the London society met Wolff at Sidon and later spoke of him as a warm-hearted missionary by whose exertions the door is fully open for proclaiming the gospel in Jerusalem among the Jews. Like the apostle Paul, the first itinerant missionary-evangelist, Wolff was often traveling, and almost always seemed to be "on the way to somewhere else" with the gospel. In the spring of 1823 he again visited Egypt in order to confirm and continue his previous work, but after a few weeks returned to Palestine. He also visited Damascus, where the Jews eagerly accepted Arabic Bibles from him, and he was well received by Jews in other cities of Syria. In 1824 he was in Baghdad where he was given a friendly and interested welcome by the Jews.

It should be noted that the countries and cities here referred to are now easily accessible by modern transport. In the early nineteenth century, however, they could be reached only on foot or by camel, and the journey was generally uncomfortable, slow, and hazardous.

At Orfa, the ancient Ur of the Chaldees, Wolff found about fifty Jewish families and some Jacobites, or Syrian Christians, claiming to be lineal descendants from Jews who received the gospel through the preaching of James in Jerusalem (the Latin equivalent of *James* is *Jacobus*).

In 1825 Wolff visited the various Jewish communities of Persia, who were then regarded as descendants of "the lost ten tribes." In the years 1827 and 1828 he went to the Greek islands and to Asia Minor. Everywhere he awakened among the Jews a widespread interest in the Christian faith. When in Bokhara in 1832 he initially encountered some opposition by local Jews who denounced him as a Russian spy. But, dressed as a Turkoman, he obtained an audience of the king. He received permission to evangelize the Jews, though he was forbidden to hold religious conversation with Moslems. By his tact and diplomacy Wolff quickly won the respect of the Jews, and during the three months of his stay he baptized twenty Jewish converts. Ten years later when Wolff visited Bokhara again, he was greeted by nearly twenty thousand people shouting, "Welcome!" During this visit he obtained permission from the king for the Jews to repair their ancient synagogue.

In 1833 Wolff was in India visiting the white and black Jews of Cochin, and the Beni-Israel of Bombay, Poona, and Calcutta. Missionaries sent by the London society had been working among these communities since 1820, but Wolff found plenty to do. In 1835 he was in Abyssinia, and in 1836 in Arabia. At Sanaa, in the Yemen, he expounded the fifty-third chapter of Isaiah to the Jews, and subsequently baptized four Jews and their families.

Wolff's zeal for propagating the gospel in far-off lands, particularly among the scattered communities of his Jewish brethren, carried him through numberless dangers, and extricated him from many perilous situations. The restlessness of his nature, which in early life impelled him to wander over Europe in search of enlightenment, developed in later years into the consecrated and impulsive energy which made him so peculiarly fitted for the role of pioneer missionary. Some compared him to David Livingstone, the great missionary-explorer. Wolff made extensive journeys among the various remnants of the then little-known communities of Jews scattered throughout Asia and Africa.

It seems that Wolff was able physically to tolerate climatic variations and extremes, and to endure exacting privations no matter how severe or sustained. The Rev. Lewis Way, vice-president of the London society, who knew Wolff well, wrote of him in *Travels and Adventures of Dr. Wolff* (vol. 1, p. 287):

> He appears to me to be a comet without a perihelion, and capable of setting a whole system on fire . . . to whom a floor of bricks is a featherbed and a box is a bolster; who makes and finds a friend alike in the persecutor of his former or of his present faith; who can concilliate a Pasha or confute a patriarch; who travels without a guide; speaks without an interpreter; can live without food and pay without money; forgiving all the insults he meets with, and forgetting all the flattery he receives; who knows little of worldly conduct and yet accommodates himself to all men without giving offense to any. . . . Such a man (and such and more is Wolff) must excite no ordinary degree of attention in a country and among people whose monotony of manners and habits has remained undisturbed for centuries. . . .

Wolff's work with the London society was terminated in 1831 and later he became vicar of Linthwaite in Yorkshire. His parochial work, however, was neither eventful nor satisfying. He had married the daughter of the earl of Oxford and they spent thirty very happy years together. Among his numerous friends were Sir Walter Scott, Alfred Tennyson, Dean Stanley, Dean Hook, and Henry Drummond after whom he named his son—who later became Sir Henry Drummond Wolff.

After his return from a second journey to Bokhara, Wolff was appointed to a little town in Somersetshire, where he remained for the rest of his life. After that time his brilliant and unique gifts found little outlet or exercise, but his energy knew no diminution. He built a new parsonage and schools, defraying a portion of the cost from the proceeds of his writings and lectures. He was as a father to the poor of his parish, and every winter he supported thirty-five families with the necessities of life.

In his *History of the London Society for Promoting Christianity Among the Jews,* the Rev. W. T. Gidney writes of Wolff:

> Wolff was essentially a missionary explorer and traveler, and held and executed a roving commission on behalf of the society. The subsequent establishment of missions to Jews in the countries which he visited was owing, in a great measure, to his early efforts, untiring energy and romantic enthusiasm. The vast stores of information about Eastern Jews, which he gathered and sent home, were of great value . . . , and the zeal which almost consumed him was at once an inspiration and an object of emulation to those who came after him. . . .

Joseph Wolff, whose wife died before him, passed away in 1862, in his sixty-seventh year. He was active in the Lord's work until the end, and his epitaph might well have been, "The zeal of Thine house hath eaten me up."

Conclusion

IT HAS BEEN shown in the preceding biographical sketches that preaching the gospel to the Jews is undeniably productive. It is not less feasible, less expedient or more difficult for Jews to be converted than it is for Gentiles to be converted.

Even if it were impossible to produce a single Jewish Christian, there would still remain the fundamental Christian duty to preach the gospel to every creature, including the Jews. And the divine order remains unchanged—it is "to the Jew first." The Jew is God's "first-born son," and he has the right of primogeniture. To the Jews first He appeared in theophanies and manifestations. To them He sent His prophets. To them He sent His Son. And to them first Christ sent His apostles.

Why "to the Jew first"? The Jews possess qualities which make them receptive to the understanding, obedience, and teaching of the laws of God. They were divinely endowed with these qualities after He chose them to be His people. Nevertheless, even these qualities failed to incline their hearts to serve God according to His will. Moses knew them to be an unstable and rebellious people (Deut. 9:24). The later prophets, especially Isaiah, denounced their wickedness. The Chronicles justified the judgment that fell upon them because of the enormity of their sins and apostasy (see II Chron. 36:15–16).

Christ was not the only one who "came unto His own" and they received Him not. The prophets and the apostles who came to their people in love and compassion were rejected. And yet, even though they were fully aware that their preaching would be rejected, they did not refrain from prophesying and preaching to the Jews. For, despite their wickedness, they were designated a holy people, a kingdom of priests, a people selected and set apart for His possession and use (cf. Exod. 19:16; Lev. 21:8; Deut. 4:7; 32:9).

There is a prófound mystery in this relation between God and His people. He visited upon them severe judgment for their sins, but He preserved them alive as a special people. And He has, indeed, a great and glorious purpose for them. They are central in His plan of salvation for mankind. In accordance with this divine plan the gospel is to be preached to them as a priority, whether they will hear or whether they will forbear (Ezek. 2:3–7; 3:7). The ultimate results of this gospel witness will be clearly visible when Christ comes for His own and to His own (cf. Isa. 2:2–3; 9:1; 40:44).

Finally, the Lord's promise and warning are to be borne in mind: "I will bless them that bless thee, and curse him that curseth thee; and in thee shall all families of the earth be blessed" (Gen. 12:3). No greater blessing can be bestowed upon the Jews by Christian believers than the preaching of the gospel, the offer of "the unsearchable riches of Christ." To withhold the gospel from them, or to hinder its proclamation merits the divine condemnation and judgment pronounced in Genesis 12:3. The Lord has set before the followers of Christ their Ebal and Gerizim, the blessing and the cursing, and it is theirs to choose. "Pray for the peace of Jerusalem." God forbid that any should sin against the Lord in ceasing to pray for the Jews!

"These all died in faith; . . . whose faith follow."
Hebrews 11:13; 13:7

DATE DUE

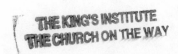